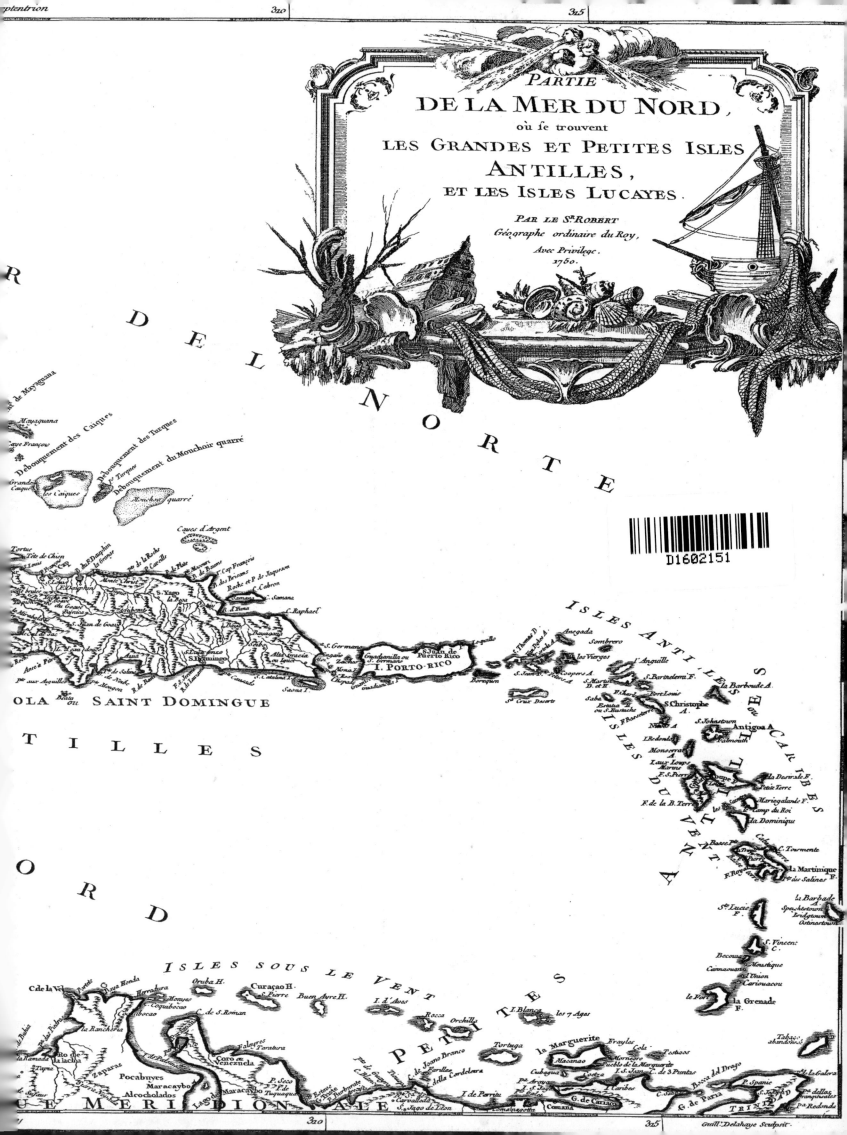

PARTIE DE LA MER DU NORD,
où se trouvent
LES GRANDES ET PETITES ISLES ANTILLES,
ET LES ISLES LUCAYES.

Par le Sr. Robert
Géographe ordinaire du Roy,
Avec Privilege.
1750.

MER DEL NORTE

I. de Mayaguana
Mayaguana
Caye François
Débouquement des Caiques
Grande Caique
les Caiques
Sr. Turque
Débouquement des Turques
Débouquement du Mouchoir quarré
Mouchoir quarré
Caues d'Argent

Tortue
Tête de Chien
S. Yago
la Bona

OLA ou SAINT DOMINGUE

C. Samana
C. Raphael

S. Germain
S. Germano
Guadeanilla ou S. Germano
S. Juan de Puerto Rico
I. PORTO-RICO
Boriquen

ISLES ANTILLES

Anegada
Sombrero
S. Thomas D.
los Vierges
l'Anguille
Coopers A.
S. Bartnelemi F.
la Barboude A.
S. Jean F.
Port Louis
S. Martin D. et H.
Saba
FiKar
Estatia ou S. Bastache
S. Christophe A.
F. Basseterre
Nieo A.
S. Johnstoun
Antigoa A.
I.Redonda
Falmouth
Monserrat A.
Laus Loups
F. S. Pierre
la Desirade F.
Paix Terre
Mariegalande F.
F. de la B. Terre
Camp du Roi
la Dominique
Basse P.
C. Tourmente
F. Roy.
la Martinique
Pta des Salines

ISLES DU VENT ou ISLES CARIBES ANTILLES

la Barbade
Spreichtetown
Bridgtown
Oestnortown
St. Lucie F.
S. Vincent C.
Becou
Moustique
Cannaouan
l'Union
Cariouacou
le Fou
la Grenade F.

TILLES

NORD

ISLES SOUS LE VENT
C. de la Vela
Aya Honda
Orua H.
Curaçao H.
S. Pierre
Buen Ayre H.
I. d'Aves
Rocca
Orchilla
I. Blanca
les 7 Ages
Herradura
Monges
Coquibocoa
C. de S. Roman
Tortuga
la Marguerite
Frayles Cols
Tesoros
Macanao
Mornearo
Pueblo de la Marguerite
I.S. Jean C. de 3 Puntas
Cubagua
Cocta
la Rancheria
Coro ou Venezuela
Arraya
S. Joano Branco
C. Codera
Caribes
Tabago abandonné
Pocabuyes
Maracaybo
Alcocholados
Lago de Maracaybo
I de Perrito
G. de Cariaco
G. de Paria
TRIN
P. Spanie
las Galera
Redondo

PETITES ANTILLES

WEST INDIAN ANTIQUE FURNITURE
of the
LESSER ANTILLES
1740–1940

DINING-ROOM INTERIOR featuring table and chairs, Barbados, *circa* 1845, and a parlour Empire armoire, Trinidad, *circa* 1820.
Collection: Haagensen House, Saint Thomas.

WEST INDIAN ANTIQUE FURNITURE
of the
LESSER ANTILLES
1740–1940

PHILIP STURM

ANTIQUE COLLECTORS' CLUB

First published 2007
© 2007 Philip Sturm
World copyright reserved

ISBN 978-1-85149-537-5

British Library Cataloguing-in-Publication Data:
A catalogue record for this book is available from the British Library

Printed in China for The Antique Collectors' Club Ltd.,
Woodbridge, Suffolk IP12 4SD

CONTENTS

THIS BOOK IS DEDICATED TO MY MOTHER AND FRIEND,
DOROTHY MARGARET WALLACE de L'ISLE STURM,
ARTIST AND CONNOISSEUR

ACKNOWLEDGEMENTS

When I decided to attempt to write a book of what I knew about Lesser Antilles furniture, I never thought it would be such an undertaking. I had a lot of help and encouragement from many different sources and quarters, with tips from numerous people and unexpected places. There have been several articles written about the subject, but always from the outside view.

The first and most important person I am grateful to is my mother Dorothy. Without her there would be no collection to write about. I also thank my brother, Maxwell G. de L'Isle Sturm, PhD, for his help in some of the grammar and editing and my sister, Baroness Mary Griendl for letting me use pieces from her collection. My thanks to all the persons throughout the Antilles from Curaçao to St Croix, namely: Eileen Bynoe, Ken Bynoe, Ross Bynoe, Michael Sheen, Dolly Blackman, Helen Campbell, Adrian Camps-Campins, Robin Maharaj, Mark Perriera, Alexandro Cummings, Lorna Bishop, David Collins, Filipe Ayala, Edith Woods, Avalino Samuels, Corrine Lockhart, Ronnie Lockhart, Gloria McGowan, Cynthia Lawrence, Kent Hughes, Sean Kravitch, Holly Reichter, Edgar Steele, Myron Jackson, Michael and Gail Ball, Elizabeth Grammar, Peggy Creque, David Knight, Aimery Caron, Brenda Sullivan, Enid Baa, Louisette Caps-Ligins, Claudette Lewis, Nancy Ayer, Gary Palmatier, Vinny Gagliani and Russell Prendergast, who spent hours typing and retyping the text.

I am also indebted to the many private residences, reference libraries, museums and archives in Trinidad, Grenada, Barbados, St Vincent, Martinique, Curaçao, St Kitts, St Thomas, St Croix and the British Museum in London, England.

Also, many thanks to all the people along the way who helped, and I may have overlooked, and all the talented people of the Lesser Antilles who inspired this book.

Finally, I should like to extend a special thank you to my photographer, Bob Coates, who has produced an outstanding range of illustrations for this book. His professionalism has contributed immeasurably to the content and appeal of the work.

INTERIOR featuring one of a pair of caned planters' chairs from Barbados, *circa* 1875. Collection: Haagensen House, Saint Thomas.

DINING ROOM INTERIOR featuring a mahogany carved and veneered sideboard, Barbados, *circa* 1870, table and chairs, Barbados, *circa* 1845, and a parlour Empire armoire, Trinidad, *circa* 1820. Collection: Haagensen House, Saint Thomas.

INTRODUCTION

This work is intended to give the reader an insight into the furniture of the Lesser Antilles, and its place in the changing politics and history of the islands.

When I began collecting West Indian antique furniture over thirty years ago there was no written book on the subject. I had to rely on general knowledge, local information and an art and history background. I spent many hours in the libraries and archives of Trinidad, Barbados, St Kitts, and the Virgin Islands and came away with very little information on furniture. The only references I got were from advertisements of furniture on packets arriving in the harbours, or from house auction sales. The inspiration for this book came from the collection formed by Dorothy Sturm, in Trinidad, during the years between 1939 and 1981. Settling in Trinidad with her husband, Dr Maxwell Gerard de L'Isle Sturm, she quickly saw the opportunity to save and collect the old furniture being discarded for more modern styles.

Soon, word got around that she was interested in 'old-time furniture' (antique furniture) and the old homes opened their doors to her. In most cases Dorothy paid fair market prices, but in other cases, four poster beds, wardrobes, and other large pieces were given away, if she would remove them. Some of the old local

Barbados mahogany tip-top tea table, c.1770.
Mahogany armchair, c.1740.

Interior showing four-poster bed and chaise longue, Barbados, *c.*1840. Mirrored wardrobe, Curaçao, *c.*1890. All mahogany.

families of diverse backgrounds and societies who did not want to keep their inherited antiques, which mostly needed restoration, would call my mother to pay a visit. Amongst the many deals she made for this furniture, she would sometimes pay for the more fashionable modern style furniture to fit out a house, in exchange for the antiques. Sometimes she would find the furniture in pieces under the old houses, and retrieve them for restoration. Soon she had so much furniture, she needed to employ a full time restorer and French polisher, giving her the opportunity to sell by auction and privately many of the pieces. This stirred up an interest in the general public, and the furniture began to be appreciated again. Another source of furniture took place after Trinidad's Independence in 1962. With many expatriates leaving the island, they would sell their possessions at auction. She would take me along, teaching me all she knew about the furniture, its origins, styles, details and how to attribute them. She also added to her collection English and French Port pieces that were representative of models used by the local craftsmen.

Dorothy graduated from the Gray School of Art in Aberdeen Scotland, which is now part of the University of Aberdeen, taking top honours and a degree in graphic and furniture design and architecture. Her judgement and knowledge of the West Indian Furniture was augmented by the information and wisdom passed to her by the artisans and master craftsmen working on the estates in Trinidad. Dorothy's initial intent was to save these pieces from oblivion, which worked its way into a large collection, requiring responsibilities. With prior tips and information, Dorothy started to make trips to Tobago, Barbados, Antigua and Grenada, acquiring more pieces. She continued adding to the collection until

her death in 1981, at which time she had in excess of two hundred pieces, not including the pieces she restored and sold over the years. This furniture was housed in 'Bagshot House', a nineteenth century estate where the family lived. At this time I inherited most of the West Indian antique furniture in the family collection, and continued her tradition of adding and restoring. This collection is by no means representative of all the furniture produced on the islands. Only six of the thirteen furniture-producing islands are in this collection but all of the forms that were used are represented. The collection in this book has been enhanced by pieces in other private collections, to try to fill in gaps of missing styles and designs. Attribution and the dating of furniture becomes difficult because the islands have changed hands so often. Styles lagged five to ten years in the colonies, where certain popular motifs remained in use long after they were fashionable in the mother countries. Some islands, like Barbados, which had a long or continuous ownership, developed a certain recognizable style. In others, where ownership had changed, the styles became intermixed. Also, early on, Barbados, Curaçao and lately Trinidad were export islands, where the free-ports (described later) played a large part in the furniture being distributed throughout the Antilles.

This leads me to believe that some of the smaller islands did not produce much furniture, and what they did produce was for local consumption. At times they used Bajan and Curaçao furniture as models for producing a more indigenous style. With this in mind, I have written the book, treating the Lesser Antilles, as a whole, emphasizing the French, English or other stylistic trends, when recognizable. The few 'labelled pieces' were used as examples, for identifying

INTERIOR.
Sitting-room showing Mahogany armoire from Martinique/Trinidad, *circa* 1870.
Collection: Adrian Camps-Campins.

Philip with a portrait of his mother, Dorothy.

BEDROOM INTERIOR (19TH CENTURY) featuring a four-poster bed from Saint Thomas, *circa* 1860, armoire from Trinidad, *circa* 1820, and dresser from Barbados, *circa* 1870. Collection: Haagensen House, Saint Thomas.

DRAWING ROOM INTERIOR featuring carved and caned Louis XVI revival sofa, *circa* 1870, from Trinidad. Collection: Haagensen House, Saint Thomas.

many of the origins and styles, in the collection. Also, Dorothy used two different schools of thought in cataloguing the furniture. First, she used the two-tier system. The first tier for the finest pieces, usually made in the town, and a second tier for country and secondary pieces. The first tier pieces were judged by their execution, decorations, material used, finish and rarity, with the second tier following everything else. She also separated the styles and overall design and finish between pre- and post-emancipation, there being a stylistic difference in the decorations between the two eras. The story of West Indian furniture needs a thorough knowledge of the styles, designs and decorations of the mother countries. In time these European forms were covered with indigenous decorations. Dorothy Sturm noted that many quality pieces of West Indian furniture left the islands.

The author hopes that this book will stimulate an interest in young West Indians to preserve their furniture heritage, in keeping it here, and returning it to the West Indies when found elsewhere. I also hope this will lead to a larger appreciation of West Indian craftsmanship and abilities.

Grouping of Louis XIV revival armchair in mahogany, Trinidad *c.*1850, with mahogany night stand, shown open and closed, Barbados, *c.*1840.

312   313   314   315   316   317

S. Jean de Portorico
P.te de l'Est
Cagade
LES ISLES VIERGES
I. Vert
S.t Thomas
Anegade ou I. Noyée
I. de Sombrero
I. de l'Anguille
les Chien
Spanish Town
Virgin Gorda
I. S.t Jean
la Coronille
I. du Nat.al
S.t Pierre
P.te de Tonnelier
I. Ginger
Pte de Sable
I. S. Martin

ISLE DE PORTORICO

I. Borquen
I. Vert
C. Rouge
P.te du N. Est
P.te des Pecheurs
P.te Espagnole
I. S. Croix
P.te de Sable
I. S. Barthelemi
le Recif
I. de la Barboude
I. do Saba
Ragged
I. de S.t Eustache
V. et F. Charles Town
la Basse Terre
P.te S.te Croix
Charles Town
St. Christophe
C. Vert
I. de Nieves
P.te Reyerson
Rade de Parham
S. Jean
Falmoul
P.te Indienne
la Redonde
P.te le Carlis
P.te Anglois
d'Antigoa

Basse Terre
I. Montferrat
p.te d'Unique
p.te du Nord
Port Louis
I. de la Desirade
le gros Morne
B.se Terre
Fort S.t Charles
P.te Noire
Fort Louis Ann.
La Petite Terre
P.te du Sud Est
des Chateaux
I. DE LA GUADELOUPE
Cabesterre
Bourg du Vieux Fort
Bourg du Baillif
P.te S.t Sauveur
I. de Marie Galante
la Basse Terre
Bourg de la B.se terre
Bourg de la Cabesterre
Isles des Saintes

P.te du Capucin
Rade du Prince Rupert
Anse du May
I. DE LA DOMINIQUE
C. François Monteur
Bourg des Roseaux
Charlotteville
P.te de Cachac
P.ta Crabes

ISLES DU VENT

I. DE LA MARTINIQUE
la Pér le
Macouba
la Trinité
Cul de Sac de la Trinité
F. S. Pierre
Cul de Sac Robert
Cul de Sac S.te François
Cul de Sac Vauclin
Fort Royal
C. Ferré
Cul de Sac S. Martin
I. des Salines

le gros Islet
Cul de Sac de l'Esperance
Anse du Choc
le Caronase
Cul de Sac
des Roseaux
Anse Mabouya
P.te Chimache
I. S.te LUCIE
le gros Piton
Cul de Sac des Savennes
Vieux Fort
Moulachique
P.te Tarrat
P.te Espagnole
p.te Tacees
Chateau Belair
Petit Bristol
Kingstown
I. S. Vincent
Hoktime
Bridgtow
P.te de Cariacou
I. de la Barbade
Becoua
Balesso
Cansouan
Isles des Moustiques

l'Union
P.te Martinique
Cariacou
Islet Rond
Islot de Levera
C. David
Morne des Sauteur
Ance Goyave
I. de la Grenade
Fort Roy
P.te du Roquin
Banc de la Grenade
P.te des Salines

CARTE DES ISLES ANTILLES ou du VENT
AVEC LA PARTIE ORIENTALE
DES ISLES SOUS LE VENT
Par M. Bonne Ingénieur Hydrographe
de la Marine

Milles Statués d'Angleterre de 69 ½ au degré.
10 20   40   60   80   100   120   140
Lieues legales de Castille de 26 ⅔ au degré.
10 20   40   60   80   100
Lieues Communes de France de 25 au degré.
5   10   20   30   40   50

Lieues Marines de 20 au degré.
5   10   15   20   25   30   35   40
Lieues de Hollande de 19 au degré.
5   10   15   20   25   30   35   40
Lieues d'Espagne de 17 ½ au degré.
5   10   15   20   25   30   35
Lieues Danoises de 13 ⅓ au degré.
5   10   15   20   25   30

Petit I. d'Aves
ou des Oiseaux

ISLES SOUS LE VENT

I. de Horchilla
I. Blanca
les Fratles
les Sœurs
les Freres
P.te Tabago
I. de la Tortuga
Isle Marguerite
la Sola
les Testigos
I. Tabago
P.te de Sabia
Rac Bay
Nicanca
Assumption
P.te le Meailloues
P.te Les Arrecifas
I. Coadera
I. Cubagua
P.te de Guacime
I. de Coche
Voare
Courenta
S. Josef
I. de Borracoa
Arzia
P.te Santo
I. DE LA TRINITE
I. de Piritú
Cumana
Cariaco
Tipirit
G. de Paria
Maporal
Tocayo
Barcelona ou Cumanagota
I. Verte

PROV. DE BARCELONA
OU DE MARACAPANA
PROV. DE CUMANA
P.te de Coar
P.te Gualuaro
R. de Venes
R. Guarapiche
les Guarauquas
P.te de la Galera

R. DE GRENADE
I. Vaya

18   17   16   15   14   13   12   11   10

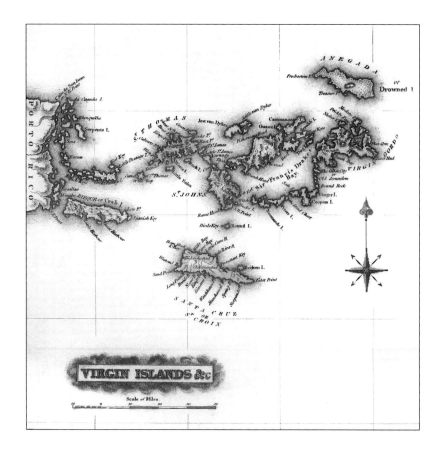

A BRIEF HISTORICAL BACKGROUND
TO THE LESSER ANTILLES

The West Indies is a crescent-shaped group of islands stretching from Cuba, close to the tip of Florida on the North American mainland, southward to Trinidad, just north of the coast of Venezuela on the South American mainland. The islands separate the Gulf of Mexico and the Caribbean Sea on the west and south from the Atlantic Ocean on the east and north. The West Indies are divided into the Greater Antilles, comprised of Cuba, Jamaica, Hispaniola (Haiti and the Dominican Republic), and Puerto Rico. The Lesser Antilles, an arch of small islands all the way down the eastern rim of the Caribbean Sea, range in size from the tiny Virgin Islands to the largest, Trinidad. These myriad shapes of green start east of Puerto Rico with St Croix, St Thomas, St John, and the British Virgin Islands of Tortola and Anguilla and St Martin, Saba, St Eustatius, St Kitts, Nevis, Antigua, Montserrat, Guadeloupe, Dominica, Martinique, St Lucia, St Vincent and the Grenadines, Grenada, Barbados, Trinidad, Tobago, Aruba, Bonaire and Curaçao.

Two main mountain chains form the Greater and Lesser Antilles. The Greater Antilles chain runs west-east while the north-south chain forms the Lesser Antilles. These mountain chains are mostly under water, and only the highest peaks form the chain of islands. They are surrounded by the Atlantic Ocean on the east, and the Caribbean Sea to the west. Many of the islands have surrounding plains and interior mountains and peaks. The West Indian climate runs from tropical to sub-tropical with semi-arid areas. The average daily temperature is

Top left. Map of the Virgin Islands.

Top right. Map of Curaçao.

Opposite. Map of the Lesser Antilles.

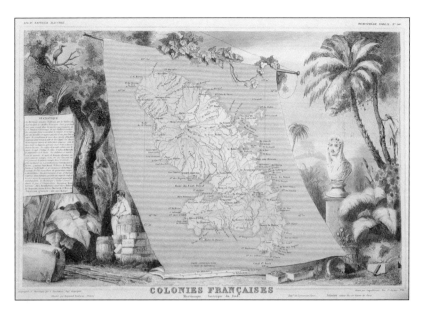

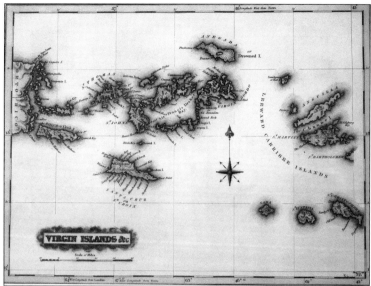

MAP

Depiction of Martinique, French West Indies, *circa* 1850.

MAP

Depiction of the Danish Virgin Islands, of Saint Thomas, Saint Croix and Saint John, and also the British Virgin Islands of Tortola, Anegada, and Anguilla. Courtesy of Michael Paiewonsky and Mapes Monde.

around 80 degrees Fahrenheit (upper 20s Celsius). During the hot season, from May to November, the temperature can rise to the low 90s (low 30s Celsius). Most islands experience a dry and wet season, annual rainfall can range from 30–90 inches, and humidity is usually high. Moisture carried by the trade winds to the Antilles provides heavy rainfall on the windward sides of the mountains and lands. The hurricane season is usually from June to November and hurricanes have caused severe damage to towns and vegetation over the years.

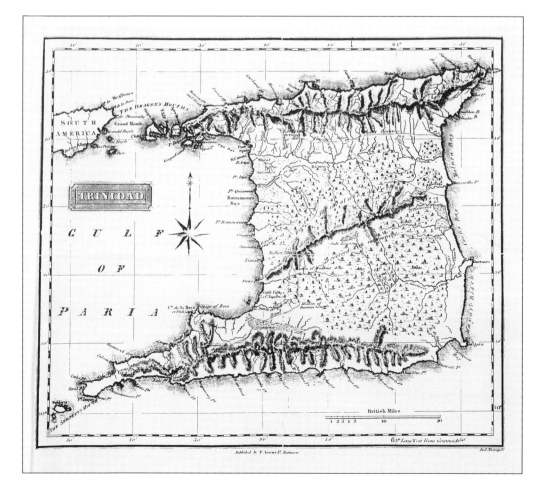

MAP

Depiction of Trinidad from around 1810. Trinidad was discovered by Christopher Columbus on his third voyage in 1492. It remained in Spanish hands until 1797, when it was taken by Colonel Ralph Abercrombie for the British in 1793. It remained a British possession, until its independence in 1962.

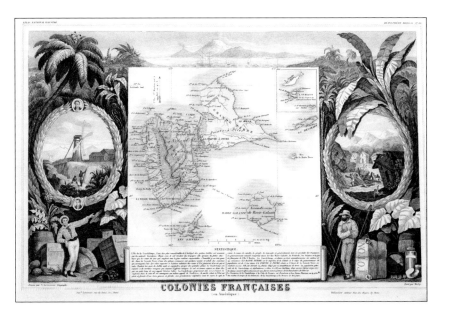

COLONIES FRANÇAISES
(en Amérique)

When Europeans first saw the West Indies it was covered with forests. They were cut down for large plantations and its timber was shipped to the mother country and also used for local construction. This resulted in the top-soil running off into the rivers and seas, causing destruction to the reefs and fish kills. This slash and burn practice of planting destroyed large tracts of the primeval forest and there are few islands left with any virgin forest. There are movements against this deforestation and many islands have passed laws protecting the ecological inheritance. Many plant species found in the Lesser Antilles, are indigenous to the area. The fauna of Trinidad and Tobago is derived from tropical South America, (Trinidad was once attached to the mainland), whereas the rest of the Antillean fauna is generally indigenous. There are agouti, lappe, deer, monkeys, pumas and ocelots. There are many species of bats and birds, including several species of parrots and humming-birds. There is also the ibis and the flamingo. The marine life is also very rich including turtles, several species of shellfish, dolphin, flying fish, among numerous other species.

The Lesser Antilles has a population that is racially heterogeneous and is largely descended from an early plantation system and society based on slavery. The population is mostly African, with East Indians, Europeans, Chinese, Arabs and others. The Africans came mostly from West Africa, the gold, ivory and slave coasts. The Europeans are descended from Spanish, French, English, Dutch and Danish colonists. The East Indians come from Bombay, Calcutta and Madras in India and the Chinese from Hong Kong and Canton. The Creole languages are formed from variants of the European languages mixed in with the African, East Indian and Chinese words and sayings. This Creole language has become the common language of many of the people, especially in the French Islands. Papiamiento, is a Spanish-Dutch-Portuguese-English Creole that is widely spoken in the Netherland Antilles. Roman Catholicism is the dominant religion of the area of the French and Spanish Antilles, while the English Islands practise Protestantism. Despite their diversity in ancestry and language, the islands of the Lesser Antilles, share a largely common culture, the result of their somewhat parallel experiences as plantation colonies. The islands take pride in their lively cultural scenes, with dances, parties and festivals, culminating in annual Carnivals.

Christopher Columbus sighted most of the Lesser Antillean islands on his second voyage in 1493 and claimed them for Spain. The indigenous Amerindians

MAP
Depiction of Guadeloupe and other French possessions in the Caribbean around 1850.

MAP
Depiction of the West Indies, by Robert de Vaugondys. Dated 1750, France.

An Amerindian family.

whom Columbus first met were the Arawaks, who originally came north from the South American continent. They began moving into the Antilles in the eighth century and by the early fifteenth century they had settled throughout the islands. They formed several groups, including the Taino of the Greater Antilles and the Igneri of the Lesser Antilles. They blended with other peace-loving peoples they met who are known as Siboney. These were pastoral people who farmed, fished and hunted small animals for survival. They lived in villages and cultivated cassava and corn. Their settlements ranged from single families to groups of 3,000 people or more and they built houses from logs with thatched roofs. These settlements were usually near rivers or the sea, as fishing was important. On Columbus' first voyage he discovered these peace-loving people were preyed upon by a tribe of cannibals who lived further to the southeast, called the Caribs. They were a warlike people who originated from the mainland of South America and had driven out most of these peace-loving settlers, shortly before Columbus arrived. At first the Indians were friendly toward the Spaniards but the latter's search and greed for gold and slaves, soon turned the natives against the newcomers.

The Amerindians suffered terribly at the hands of the Spaniards. They were enslaved and died in their thousands as a result of the harsh treatment they received and from European diseases, such as influenza, smallpox and chickenpox, against which they had no immunity. The Spaniards hunted the Indians with dogs, and fought wars with soldiers on horseback, a sight the Indians had never encountered before. They thought the horse and mounted soldier was one living creature and together with guns and steel swords the Indians did not stand a chance. In the beginning, they were sometimes able to drive the Europeans back to their ships by sheer weight of numbers, but this was only temporary. Their enemies soon overwhelmed them and on many occasions the Indians committed suicide in their thousands, throwing themselves and their families off high cliffs into the sea, rather than being enslaved. They had no writing and have left very little as to their way of life.

Their settlements comprised a large collection of huts without streets and the chief living in the largest hut. Their buildings were circular, with a cone-shaped roof of thatched grass and palm fronds, supported by a central post. This configuration is similar to other residences found throughout the Antilles and good reconstructions can be found in the Antiguan Museum in St John. There were also hexagonal and rectangular structures. These various shelters are called *carbets, ajoudas* and *canayes* by the Spaniards. These houses were sometimes grouped around a ball court or central plaza where the cooking was done. All these buildings were simple and strong, standing up to the high winds of the hurricanes.

After 1542, Spain finally granted the Indians their full freedom, but the Encomienda System, (where groups of 50–300 Indians were used as slaves on plantations, under the supervision of a Cacique or Indian Chief, whose duty was to Christianize and Europeanize them), killed them off in their hundreds, and at a time when their survival was already in serious decline. For the indigenous Indian it was too late. The Spaniards married into what was left of the Indian population, (as Spanish women were not brought to the Antilles), and this produced a Mestizo population. After a while the pure Indian disappeared from the Antilles, with a small colony left on a reservation in Dominica.

An Amerindian ceremony to raise courage.

Amerindians repelling Europeans.

General view of St Croix.

The islands of the Lesser Antilles were neglected by Spain for the larger ones of the Greater Antilles, Panama and Mexico because of the gold found there. For almost one hundred and fifty years after the Spanish conquest, these Lesser Antillean islands were ignored, except as bases for pirates and privateers. These pirates were covertly supported by their various Kings, targeting the Spanish galleons, and transitory or short-lived settlements of the Dutch, English and French. Permanent agricultural settlements followed these trading and raiding posts in the early seventeenth century. In 1600 the Dutch settled in St Eustatius, and in 1605 the English attempted a settlement on Grenada. Between 1624 and 1640, St Kitts, Nevis, Barbados, Antigua, Montserrat, and St Lucia were settled by the English, Saba and St Martin by the Dutch and Martinique and Guadeloupe by the French. In 1625 the English and Dutch settled St Croix, but these settlements did not last and St Croix was under the rule of the French, the Knights of Malta, and the Spanish for short periods until permanent settlement by the Danes in 1733. St Thomas was settled by the Danes in 1672, and they took control of St John in 1718. Nearby Tortola was first settled in 1648 by the Dutch. In the early 1600s the Spanish established a settlement in Trinidad. These islands went through many rulers and changes because of European wars of the seventeenth and eighteenth centuries and the many treaties that evolved from them.

Tobacco production.

After the discovery and two or three generations of settlement, small farms produced indigo, tobacco, and other staples such as cassava and corn. These were exported to the mother countries in exchange for material goods such as cloth, tools and other iron implements. Sugar was produced by Portugal on their islands in the Azores and Madeira via Africa, and introduced into Brazil in the early 1600s. From there the Dutch learned the process and provided the knowledge to the Antilles where it became the main crop, turning the islands from small farms to large plantations. The first island to become completely covered with sugar plantations was Barbados. As this sugar plantation system needed a lot of labour, and the local Indian populations were decimated, the Europeans turned to indentured labour. It became apparent, after the first twenty years of settlement, that the European powers had to look elsewhere for their

Sugar plantation.

manpower to operate large scale plantations. African slavery was not yet tapped into, to any large degree, and the nearest manpower at hand was the mother countries' convict population. The jails in Europe were emptied and the worst of humanity were sent to the islands as indentured servants or slaves. The worst offenders, such as rapists, murderers and traitors were sold to the estate owners and put into the fields for life. The lesser offenders, such as thieves and debtors, were used in the production of buildings, coppering, wheel-wrighting and furniture-making. These lesser criminals were given a time period to serve, and were rewarded with a small parcel of land, or could purchase their freedom from their masters. Another large source of European slaves came from the defeated Irish and Scottish armies during their seventeenth and eighteenth century wars with England.

The homeless from the European Thirty Years' War, came voluntarily to the Antilles as indentured servants and secured positions in and about the households of their respective masters. These indentured men sometimes were left to run the plantations in their owners' absence, and many were exceedingly cruel to their wards and especially to the slaves under them. It was not long before it was discovered that large plantations needed much more labour than Europe could provide, and the European slaves could not last in the fields. They died off like flies under the hot sun and the ill-treatment and many who were under an African boss were ill-treated and derided worse than slaves. They wore knickers, a shirt and hat, and in bending over to till the soil, the backs of their legs got burned and red from the sun. This lead to them being called 'red legs', especially in Barbados, a name which has stuck to their descendants up to this day. When they did secure their freedom, they moved in to the towns and earned a living as porters and clerks. They eventually became part of the society, marrying into the black population, which was imported into the Antilles to replace them in the fields.

The demand for sugar in Europe was so great that all the available land was given over to this rich cash crop. It could be grown by unskilled labour, but demanded skilled technical knowledge of the equipment which France and England did not have, and such help could only come from the Dutch. The Dutch had plantations in Brazil and ruled the seas, replacing the Spaniards in the Antilles. After the Portuguese threw the Dutch out of Brazil, they had good reasons to build up the Antilles' sugar plantations systems, so they could carry on their sea trading. They had the knowledge and experience from Brazil and could supply the equipment and technology from Europe. Therefore, it would be correct to say that the Dutch were the founders of the sugar plantation systems on the French and English Islands.

The first sugar canes were planted in Barbados in 1637 by one Pieter Brower, a Dutchman. At first the cane was just squeezed and sent back as juice to be manufactured in the Mother Countries, but this was not a great success. In 1642, the Dutch provided rollers, coppers and other equipment on credit, against the first crop, hence sugar manufacturing began in Barbados. A contemporary account of around 1645 describes the situation. French Guadeloupe had its first successful factory in 1647, again with the help of the Dutch. France offered better terms to attract indentured servants (engagees) for three years. There were already some African slaves in the French Islands but the flood from Africa had not yet started, due to the indentured slaves and servants from Europe. Sugar became the only crop of importance in the English and French Islands by 1650

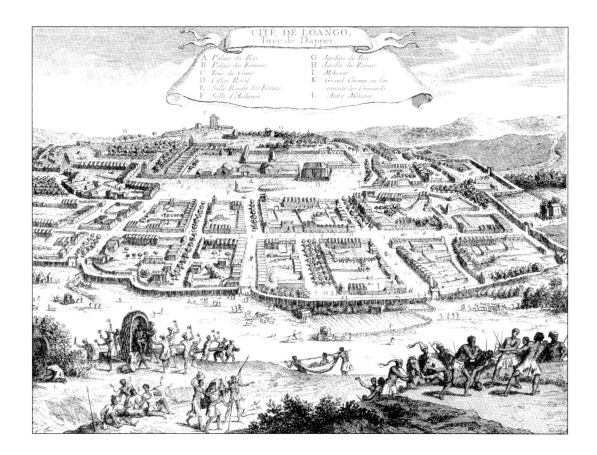

and it was to change the whole racial, political and social structure of the islands.

City of Loango.

By now the islands had become large sugar plantations and these establishments needed a large disciplined work force and as no land remained to grant to indentured labourers, this labour dwindled and ceased. All methods of propaganda in Europe became useless and only the most desperate war refugees came to the West Indies where there might be a chance of improving their lives. Even the English Civil War prisoners, the Irish who were not massacred at Progheda and the followers of the hapless Duke of Monmouth, were not enough to help these plantations succeed. These prisoners who did not cost the planters anything were treated worse than the African slaves, as they were not looked upon as a monetary investment. In 1647, the English historian Ligon writes 'I have seen such cruelty there done to servants, as I do not think one Christian could have done to another.'

By the late 1630s the Dutch had seized most of the Portuguese slave Barracoons or holding forts in West Africa, as a way of keeping their naval empire prospering. They would sell the slaves to the West Indies as the demand was increasing for labour on the plantations, as sugar planting spread and white labour declined. This was the opportunity for the Dutch to get in to the slave trade. First, it was a small amount, but as time passed it became a shameless trade in human cargo Barbados did have a few African slaves in 1640, but by 1645 there were more than 6,000 Africans and 40,000 Europeans. In 1670, however, the Africans outnumbered the Europeans by 45,000 to 20,000 and by 1700 there were four Africans to each European. This continued throughout the Lesser Antilles until, by the early eighteenth century, the African population was by far the largest group in the French and English Islands. The Europeans developed a garrison and seige mentality under these conditions, becoming ever more paranoid and cruel and stringent measures were used to discourage any rebellions.

The markets for the African slaves were mostly from the west coast of Africa. Among the countries were Sierra Leone, the Grain, the Ivory, the Gold and the Slave Coasts. Also, the Niger Delta, Cameroon, Gabon and Loango. These

King Mono-Motapa.

'The most important king "Mono-Motapa", most powerful and so rich he is called the "Emperor of Gold". He has several kings that pay tribute to him. They occupy lower Ethiopia, and their children are brought up in his palace, in order to keep their fathers under his control. This kingdom is very large and its circumference is about 2,400 miles. He wages war against Prete Jay, Emperor of Cabbising. He keeps his court in Zimbabwe where he has his ordinary guard, his wives and 200 dogs, big and nasty. The account of the year 1631 tells us that this king, "Mono-Motapa", had been baptized with all his court by the Jesuit Fathers. This king is served only by people on their knees, there are in this kingdom, women who go to war and are as good as men, in his armies there are large numbers of elephants, lots of sugar, several gold mines. These people are black, courageous, and so well-trained that they can outrun horses. The idolaters, sorcerers, adulterers, and scoundrels are instantly punished.'

people had many traits in common and shared languages from the Sudanic or Bantu tribes. The Kings in these areas who sold slaves to the Europeans through Muslim Arab middlemen, were of the Fanti-Ashanti, the Dahomeans, the Yoruba and the Bini of Nigeria, amongst others. It must be noted that when the Africans were brought to the Antilles no differences were made between King, Chief, Artisan or Slave. All Africans were stripped of their belongings but not their knowledge or talent, so in this diaspora you had naturally talented leaders, cultivators, woodworkers, stonecutters, and so on.

Slavery had long existed throughout the region with plantations of sugar cane and other crops in Dahomey and in the Niger Delta. Slavery in Africa and the ancient worlds of Egypt and Greece were a form of domestic servitude usually to repay some family debt or prisoners taken in inter-tribal warfare. It was by no means the same as chattel-slavery, where they were valuable assets used to trade for guns, cloth, hardware, etc. After being captured and traded, they were marched to the coast in yokes, confined in coastal forts or baracoons, then packed tightly in ships for the trip to the Antilles. Many died on this horrific middle passage and for 300 years ten million Africans were transported in this way. Subjection was maintained by the savage use of force – dismemberment, mutilation, and torture – and, as items of property, their bondage was also extended to their offspring. Their owner was all-powerful and the source of everything. Many, however, opposed their enslavement by calculated idleness, wilful carelessness and feigned stupidity. They deliberately destroyed the slave owners' property, they rebelled, rose up and fought back. Many ran away and formed communities in the forests and the mountains. They even fought the British and French to a standstill, forcing treaties with the

King Tombut, King of Guinea.

'The most important and fearsome of black Africa in the western territories of Ethiopia, from the Atlantic to beyond the Senegal River. He is so powerful that he can send to war as many as 300,000 men which makes him feared to the point that he gets tributes from other kings, his neighbours, of their goodwill, otherwise he gets it by force. His strength is noted by his ordinary guard which has more than 3,000 gentlemen and knights, and a large number of footmen who use poisoned arrows when at war. He keeps many doctors, but he is a silent enemy of Jews. These people are black, of gentle persuasions, good runners, jumpers, strong, skilful and very courageous in their kind of war.'

VUE EST du CAP CORSE, desiné en 1727 par Smith.

Slave holding fort in Africa.

European Nations. These people were called 'maroons' and the communities 'maroonages'. Many rebellions were put down with brutal repression, but none so destructive to life and property as the rebellion of the Africans against the French, that lead to the Independence of St Dominique, now Haiti. Here, in 1803, the Africans defeated the French colonial government, the English, Spanish and French national armies, winning their freedom and independence. In Danish St John the slaves captured and held the island for six months although the rebellion was eventually put down by soldiers of the French Army in Martinique.

As the eighteenth century drew to a close, awareness of the evils of slavery started to rise in the capitals of Europe. In England, Dr Samuel Johnson who produced the original English dictionary, proposed a toast 'to the next rebellion in the Antilles'. Founded in the seventeenth century by George Fox, the first and most important group of anti-slavery humanitarians were known as the Quakers and also as the 'Society of Friends'. In 1676, they were the first group in the Americas to free their slaves. The Quakers in the islands were not so lucky as they were few in number and were soon chased off by the majority Anglican and Catholic slave owners. In 1727, they campaigned against the slave trade in England, and made laws within their religious group against the trade, expelling anyone who would not adhere to them. Another person to rise up against the slave trade was Granville Sharp who worked hard to eliminate the laws of slavery in England. He wrote a pamphlet, 'A Representation of the Injustice and Dangerous Tendency of Tolerating Slavery in England'. After many court cases, in 1772 the courts of England finally found 'the claim of slavery can never be supported', according to the English laws.

In 1787, the Quakers formed an anti-slavery society, naming it 'The Committee for the Abolishment of the Slave Trade'. The Committee had the support of the Prime Minister, William Pitt the Younger, who asked William Wilberforce to be his representative. Wilberforce called slavery 'an affront to God and below the dignity of civilized people'. He had large support from many industrialists, especially after it was attested that revenue from taxes from imported cotton, and the export of manufactured goods, brought in much more tax than the profits of the slave trade. Success was not quick, as West Indian interests had many seats in

Great House or Plantation House.

A sugar plantation

Parliament, and were backed by Members whose living came from the slave trade. After several bills in 1789 and 1791 to abolish the trade were turned down, Wilberforce was finally successful in 1792 when the House of Commons agreed to abolish the trade by 1796. The following year England went to war with France and the Bill was put on the back burner until 1806, when Pitt died. He was succeeded by Charles James Fox in 1806 an avid abolitionist, and the Abolition Act was passed into law in 1807 and the slave trade was ended on 1st January, 1808. Several nations followed England's example: Holland in 1814, France in 1818 and Spain in 1820. Abolitionists believed slavery would end with the outlawing of the trade but this did not happen. The colonial assemblies continued using piracy to import slaves and took better care of the slaves' offspring. However, all this was in vain as the end of the slave trade announced the end of slavery – it was just a matter of time.

The best estate land was devoted to sugar, some of it to freshly planted cane, the rest to ratoons grown from cane stalks cut in previous years. On the remainder, draft animals were pastured, slaves' provisions grown and trees cut for building and for fuel to run the factory. The cluster of stone factory buildings: mill, boiling house, curing house and rum distillery was often substantial. Ruins of these buildings, especially the mill, can be seen on most West Indian islands. Other buildings were slave huts, storerooms, workshop and most important the Great House, where the master and his family lived. Sometimes when he was absent, either back in Europe, or in the town, he would leave a trusted indentured servant in charge. They ran the business of planting and reaping the sugar cane for the planters who stayed most of the year in Europe.

Some owners did not build a Great House, and stayed in the bookkeeper's house when visiting the plantation. The early Great Houses were built to a fairly simple two-storey design. The bottom storey was made of stone or brick, and was used either as a storage area, hurricane shelter, or even a stronghold in case of pirate attacks or slave revolts. They were also sometimes armed to fight off other European enemy attacks. The top storey was sometimes of wood or stone and the roof was tiled. These plantation and town houses were roofed with red fish scale terracotta tiles, slate or shingles. The terracotta tiles were made in kilns in the

PAINTING.
  Depiction of Bagshot House, Maraval, Trinidad. British West Indies, *circa* 1900.

Port St George in Grenada.

Old photograph of typical veranda, c.1900.

French Islands and exported up and down the chain of the Lesser Antilles to the various free-ports. All the old paintings and prints of these parts attest to these red roof towns in the islands. These roofs were supported by imported pine rafters, beams and lathes, and were sometimes weakened and or destroyed by termite infestation, coupled with hurricanes and earthquakes.

With the invention of galvanized or tin roofing it was less costly and more efficient (terracotta tiles absorbed water before there was a run off) to repair or replace these tiles with sheets of galvanized, and wherever this took place the galvanized was painted red to match the remaining tiles. Hence there are red painted galvanized roofs in most of these towns that originally had red tiles (in Charlotte Amalie, Saint Thomas there are two of the original roofs left, one with three-quarters of the hip roof in tiles and the other quarter being galvanized, and one with its roof of slate). These conditions can be found throughout the Antilles, especially in the town of St George in Grenada. Slate came from Europe, mainly England, as ballast, and was readily available throughout the free-ports. The British Islands almost entirely used slate, but in English Trinidad the roofs were mixed because of the French influence. Also in the Danish West Indies there was a mixture of all three different roofings because of the free-port of Charlotte Amalie. Wooden shingles were mostly used on smaller houses as roofing and sidings.

Most vernacular architecture had shingle roofs painted red as was the custom. The Dutch Islands used tiles in their colonies, importing them mostly from Venezuela making their roofs look like those in Spanish South American Colonial Towns. The staircase was usually on the outside connecting with a veranda, which usually ran around the top and bottom storeys. These verandas became a favorite place for living and entertaining as they were the most breezy place in the house. At times these estate houses were small, one storey of wood on a raised stone basement, and other times they were large and beautifully designed and had fabulous interiors of mahogany and other rare woods. In some cases, no expense was spared, as can be seen in Sam Lord's Castle in Barbados (*circa* 1820), or in Clarence House (*circa* 1790), built for the Duke of Clarence (the future William IV of England) in Antigua. These were beautiful settings for the furniture you see in this book.

Some of the houses were very grand with mahogany floors, staircases, panelling, doors and mouldings. The rooms inside usually consisted of a large central hall which was used as the sitting room, dining area, office, banqueting or dance hall. The surrounding rooms were bedrooms and as a rule, all of these rooms opened out on to the veranda. High ceilings and large doors and windows helped keep the house cool, as it was the custom to place the house on one of the breeziest hills of the plantation. Also placed on these high elevations were the

Old photograph of estate house interior, *c*.1900.

27

PRINT.
View of Charlotte Amalie, Saint Thomas from the outlying Hassel Island, Virgin Islands, *circa* 1850.

PRINT.
View of Charlotte Amalie, St Thomas, Virgin Islands, Danish West Indies, *circa* 1875.

PRINT.
Two early views of the island of Saint Croix showing a part of the towns of Christianssted and Fredericksstted. Saint Croix is the largest of the US Virgin Islands. During its history it has been colonised by Spain, Great Britain, the Netherlands, France, the Knights of Malta and Denmark. The island was purchased from Denmark by the United States in 1917.

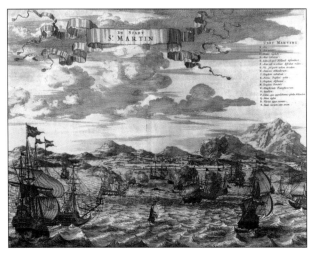

PRINT.
Spanish ships enforcing a siege of the Dutch settlement on the island of Saint Martin (Sint Maarten) in 1633. The island is now administered jointly by the Netherlands and France.

PRINT.
View of Saint Pierre, Martinique, French West Indies, prior to its destruction by volcanic eruption in 1904, *circa* 1875.

Petit-Sturm House   Governor's Residence

windmills for grinding the cane. The kitchen was usually in a separate building, to minimize the chance of fires. The servants and slave quarters were also in a separate area of the plantation, but within full view of the Great House. Another reason for placing the Great House on a high elevation was to be away from the noise of the work yard and the slave village. This position also gave the owner a good view of the surrounding area, in case of trouble or disturbances. By the end of the eighteenth century, sugar plantations with large scale African slavery, had spread to almost every island in the Lesser Antilles.

Each island in the Lesser Antilles has its special features, a unique self-image and a particular view of the others. Islanders insist on these differences as a matter of local pride. These islands developed along European, Indian and African economic and social lines but their religion, language and sociological input were different. In Martinique, for example, a French Catholic heritage of cuisine, carnival and dress, was mixed with an African voodoo heritage producing a French-Creole Society. This heritage produced a language, cuisine and attitude in the people. These same Martiniquans moved to Trinidad during the French Revolution, taking their indigenous culture, and mixing it with Spanish/Indian or Mestizo culture. This, in turn, produced a hybrid local culture that has recognizable French, Spanish, Indian and African traits in the language, food, dance, design and the overall culture of the Trinidadian. In 1797, the British took Trinidad from the Spanish, and added another cultural input to this already melting pot. All of these mixtures of race, religion, food, dance and festivals are

PHOTOGRAPH.

Image of hillside of Charlotte Amalie St Thomas showing 'Catherineberg' the Governor's residence. This hill was constructed during the early nineteenth century and also shows the stone-constructed Petit-Sturm House. The Petit family were Creoles from Dominica. Rachel Petit was the mother of Camille Pissaro, who was born in St Thomas in the 1830s, and is known as the 'Father of French Impressionism'. The photograph was taken around 1970.

recognized by each island as what makes them individual, and, at the same time, produces a unifying culture.

This sort of pot-pourri is evident throughout the Lesser Antilles to a lesser or greater degree, depending on the island's background and development. As diverse as they are, however, they are in many ways similar. Resemblances from island to island are substantial and durable. Even though social structure and way of life varies from place to place, their basic forms persist throughout the Caribbean. European colonial heritage, including slavery, transcends territorial boundaries. The physical landscapes, social structures and ways of life are in a large measure plantation by-products. Sugar not only caused West Indian territories to resemble each other, it unified them. This aspect throughout the Antilles was known as the 'Sugar Culture'. Once these islands were made over to the 'King of Crops' – sugar, the system was all the same. Large plantations with Indian, European and African slavery was the common denominator throughout. There was a great movement of the planters to spread their holdings from island to island. This produced families of the owners and slaves being dispersed throughout the Antilles, so that one large family could have members owning plantations on several islands, spreading their ideas and policies throughout these islands. Soon these planters and their slaves spoke a Creole language that only they could understand from island to island. When a West Indian territory exchanged one European master for another, its planters, slaves, merchants and even officials, carried on regardless. For example, the eighteenth century conquests by the British of Dominica, St Lucia and Trinidad left most of the French landowners undisturbed.

The Seven Years' War, (this war and its peace is basically the reason for the political makeup of the Antilles until the Independence movements in the 1960s) between England and France (1756-63) began in Europe and North America, and was fought to secure English North America by seizing French-Canada. At the start, the French captured the English island of Minorca and the English retaliated by taking Cape Breton Island with its important French fortress, Louisbourg, Canada. These were taken to be used as pawns at the peace table, as were each others' undefended islands in the Lesser Antilles. The planters of the English islands began to think that their possessions would be safer if the French islands became British, at least during the war. In 1758, England confident of success in Europe, attacked the French West Indies. This confidence was upheld by England's defeat of the French navy in the Mediterranean. They seized Guadeloupe in 1759 and the French Islands were given favourable terms and surrendered quietly.

In 1762, Spain joined France against England. The same year England's Admiral Rodney sailed out of England with a large fleet, into the Caribbean, and with a detachment was able to blockade the French Fleet in Cap Francis, San Dominique in the Greater Antilles. He then moved down to the Lesser Antilles, capturing Saint Lucia, Saint Vincent and Martinique. Dominica had already surrendered to an English-American force in 1761 and Tobago was occupied around the same time. All the French possessions in the Lesser Antilles were now in English hands. The English were now eager for peace and these captured islands were used as pawns in the demands of the French, English and for the reciprocal demands in Europe. England's first objective was to safeguard their

American colonies and French-Canada had to be kept. However, as Canada was a wilderness and its economic value was smaller than Martinique's, Canada was given over to England and France got back its Antilles' sugar islands. This goes to show how economically valuable sugar was in the mid-eighteenth century. Many people in England wanted to keep Guadeloupe as it was very profitable, but France prevailed. The peace came to a compromise, the English getting Canada, Grenada, St Vincent, Tobago and the whole of North America east of the Mississippi. The French retained Guadeloupe, Martinique and St Lucia, and Spain, for helping France, got the French colony of Louisiana. The disputes were settled but set the stage for the further wars of Independence. The great superiority of the English in the Caribbean at this time, failed to unite the greater part of the West Indies and North America under one flag. Sugar prices in the Antilles started to drop as the European market was flooded by cheaper sugar from Cuba and Brazil, then the discovery of beet sugar in Europe all rang the economic death knell for the smaller islands of the Antilles. After all sorts of schemes to prolong slavery, such as, amelioration, apprenticeship, support for the free coloureds and several uprisings, the end was near. A new reformed House of Commons in England met in January in 1833 and voted for the immediate end of slavery. It was enacted on 1st August, 1834, followed by France and Denmark in 1848, the Dutch in 1865 and the Spanish in 1886.

Free-ports were an interesting feature of the Lesser Antilles. Colonies belonging to a European power were not allowed to trade with any other European Country or colony unless by treaty. These Europeans were usually at war or odds with each other, so to facilitate their growing sea trade they opened up certain ports to all nations and their colonies. The French opened free-ports in Martinique and Guadeloupe in 1763, and St Lucia in 1767. The British Free-port Acts of 1766

PRINT.
View of Bridgetown, Barbados, British West Indies, by Coyens, *circa* 1650.

opened two free-ports in Dominica at Rosseau and Prince Rupert's Bay. By the mid-1700s, the Danish in St Thomas and the Dutch in Curaçao and St Eustatius became free-ports. These free-ports opened up the Caribbean as never before. Free trade now allowed goods such as furniture made in Curaçao, St Thomas, America, Europe to be shipped and bought by all of the Caribbean islands through these free-ports This traffic in locally made furniture was abundant and widespread. Free-ports conducted business with persons from all over the Caribbean, and the world. Many planters changed islands in search of richer soil or better prospects. Many held or owned properties in two or more islands. They took their customs, and sometimes their household belongings, including furniture with them from one island to the other. After emancipation, labourers and artisans also travelled between the islands, looking for employment. Linkages of persons, things and ideas have persisted throughout West Indian history and lend the whole Caribbean area a special unity.

After emancipation the days of unpaid labour were over and the colonial powers introduced the system of apprenticeship. This apprenticeship was supposed to train the ex-slave to enter the free society and take care of himself, but this did not work. As well-intended as it might have been for the former slave, it was seen as another way to keep him in bondage. This did not last very long and together with uprisings, missionaries and abolitionists, freedom was granted outright five years after the Emancipation Act of 1833 in the British Islands with the other countries following thereafter. Most ex-slaves did not want to go back to work on the plantations unless there was absolutely no other option. Where there was a need for labour in the town, this was where most of the free men moved. However, when there were no jobs the ex-slaves that stayed on the plantation proved to be good workers. Antigua was the only island that did not try the apprenticeship system. The slaves there were freed outright by the local government and within three months, three quarters of the ex-slaves were working as free paid labourers. This happened as there was no free land in Antigua for the ex-slaves to buy or occupy. This experiment in Antigua proved that free men could work better than slave labour because within ten years Antigua was producing twice the amount of sugar as before emancipation.

Some islands had available land and some labourers were able to save to buy plots and live off their crops, and some formed communities in the hills and on Crown Lands. Only Trinidad in the Lesser Antilles had a lot of available land and it was here that maroon communities were formed. The planters feared that they would be faced with no labour force or be ruined by high wages. Many left, but those that stayed got together with the governments to find a way to get inexpensive and permanent labour. Trinidad, where the labour problems were desperate, turned to importing cheap labour from the British Isles, with Irish, Scottish and Northern European immigration, but this failed as many died and in the end most asked for repatriation. Labourers in the island of Madeira, where there was a large cheap work force on the sugar plantations, were brought to the West Indies between 1835 and 1882. Here again, this scheme was unsatisfactory from early on as the death rate was too high. Free Africans were also imported from Sierra Leone from 1841 to 1862. This scheme also failed because promises to the Africans were not kept and they were treated badly. They next turned to Chinese immigration which lasted a long time from 1806–93. Thousands of

Chinese labourers were imported into the islands from the Portuguese colony of Macao. These immigrants were convicts and prisoners and there were no women. Again false promises chased the Chinese off the fields and into the towns where they thrived as small shopkeepers. As China was not a British colony immigrants were a costly and time consuming deal as the Chinese and Portuguese Governments made greater demands.

England and France then turned to India where they had colonies and ports respectively and this was the beginning of a large scale immigration of indentured labour to the West Indies, where today they make up the majority of the population in Trinidad. The great flood started in 1838. They were drawn from the poor in the cities of Bombay, Calcutta and Madras. The British also allowed the French, Dutch and the Danes to import the Indians, so today we have Indian populations throughout the Caribbean. The West Indies imported some 416,000 immigrants by the time they stopped the scheme in 1917. This immigration appeared successful as the economy of the Lesser Antilles did have a resurgence in the 1840–50s. However, this was not always so as things were changing all the time and the entire nineteenth century, from 1830–1917, was an up and down situation, as new forces were continually introduced into the islands. One of these forces was the planting of alternative crops. Most of these crops were not new to the West Indies, some being indigenous and some being export crops before sugar.

Sea island cotton was exported from Barbados in the 1600s. By 1724 Montserrat, Antigua, Nevis and St Kitts all exported cotton. Between 1784 and 1802, 70% of the cotton imported into Europe came from the West Indies. It had

Willemstad, Curaçao. General view.

St Christopher with Nevis in the background.

an economic revival in the early twentieth century and it is still produced today. Coffee was introduced into the Antilles by the Spaniards and has been grown in Trinidad since the 1600s. Dominica, St Vincent and Grenada also used it as an alternative crop. Cocoa was another plant native to South America that was introduced by the Spaniards and is still grown widely in the Antilles. When the sugar industry declined in the 1830–40s cocoa was given priority by the planters. In the Lesser Antilles cocoa, coffee, limes, cotton, arrowroot, ginger, indigo, pimiento, tobacco, sugar and lumber were the main export crops by 1870. Rice was introduced by the Chinese and Indian populations in Trinidad and it is still cultivated today. Limes were produced in Dominica, St Lucia and Montserrat, rubber was planted in Trinidad in 1864 followed by coconut plantations between 1914 and 1921. Nutmeg and other spices are produced today in Grenada and St Vincent. Bananas were introduced into the islands by the Spaniards in 1516, and became an instant popular food. It was not used as an export item until the late nineteenth century and became a success, especially for the small land owner.

By 1896, with the exception of bananas, the other crops were not a huge economic success. Diseases and droughts killed off the limes in St Lucia and Dominica, and the cocoa and cotton plants also suffered from boll worm disease. The West Indies were greatly disadvantaged by these disasters and adverse market forces. The rubber industry failed against cheaper produce from Malaysia, and the cocoa planters could not compete with Ghana's output which dominated the market. A lot of natural disasters and factors came together with the loss of

markets and destroyed opportunities by the 1930s. Great hardships were produced within the Antilles at this time and only Trinidad survived as it had oil and a natural pitch lake. Many West Indian people from the small islands migrated to Trindad and the Panama Canal for work and the opportunities it offered.

Throughout all of the nineteenth century, furniture making had its good and bad years. Furniture designs still followed the mother country right up to Independence in the 1960s. By the nineteenth century the different woods were being cultivated for export and local usage. By 1800, Barbados started to harvest its mahogany plantations which it had planted in the 1780s, but it still had to import from Jamaica and Honduras. Trindad also started to plant large plantations of different lumber producing trees. The trade between the islands and the Americas fluctuated according to the markets. Furniture was still being moved up and down the Antilles chain as always, but now there was a lot more movement. Faster and larger transportation made it easier and there were more furniture stores selling imports from all over the West Indies, the Americas and Europe. Today these same pieces of furniture are in great demand, especially the pieces of the eighteenth and nineteenth centuries, and some of the fine pieces that were made on a large scale in the early twentieth century. By now veneer was no longer used and the furniture of the '30s and '40s was made of solid precious woods. The trade still survives today but mostly as restorers and custom builders. It seems the last large-scale production of quality pieces made in the Antilles date from the 1940s, and are still plentiful.

St Vincent. View of Porto-Grande from Kingstown.

A Brief Historical Background to the Furniture of the Lesser Antilles

from the Virgin Islands to Trinidad and Curaçao

The indigenous inhabitants of the Lesser Antilles, the Taino, Carib and Arawak Indians, have left little evidence of their furniture, except for some ceremonial stools which can be seen in collections and museums in the larger islands of the Greater Antilles, such as Cuba and Puerto Rico. In all the different tribes' homes, their furnishings were simple. They included wooden stools, baskets and hammocks, the hammock being indigenous to them. Among the Indian furniture that has survived, are the 'Duhos' (ceremonial stools), used by the Caciques (Chiefs), and the Shamans (Priests). The Duho was a low stool with four feet carved from wood or stone. They were sometimes decorated with shell and gold inlay and appliqués, and sometimes had elaborately carved backs. They were highly prized and are still used today by Shamans in South America. Surviving stools have been found in caves, hidden from the Spaniards, as these stools were considered holy and prized above gold and silver. They were usually made from the wood of ebony, mahogany and lignum-vitae. The carving on these stools usually represented the figures of their Gods, or 'Zemi'. When found by the Spaniards, they were considered idols and destroyed or buried. It is surprising that any have survived. Other designs on these stools were zoomorphic with swirls and leaf designs, and there is historical reporting by the Spaniards that these stools were made by both male and female artisans. Very little of the Indian material culture has survived, such as their woven garments, hammocks, and plaited baskets. Quite a lot of their jewellery of jade, stone carvings and pottery has survived, which shows us their mastery of design and expression of pageantry used on public occasions and important appearances.

In the late 1400s when Christopher Columbus came upon the islands of the Lesser Antilles and claimed them for Spain, there were ship carpenters aboard. It is known these carpenters stayed on the islands to build when Columbus left. When the colonists settled on these islands, more artisans and carpenters were with them who trained the Indians in the European manner. There was already much talent among the Indians, as Columbus had found in their villages and the construction of their huts and houses. The Spaniards would have learned about the different woods and their uses from the indigenous peoples, and would have taken back examples for their sponsors, the King and Queen of Spain. The contact between the Spanish and the Indians varied from island to island. At first the Indians were in awe of the Spanish and welcomed them as Gods. However, as soon as the Spanish started to treat them as savages, the mood of the Indians turned ugly. This news was quickly spread to the other islands, where Columbus and his men were greeted with spears and arrows. From then on, Columbus had to defeat the local populations as he moved up the chain of the Lesser Antilles. He did not make any settlements on the smaller islands, bypassing them as his expeditionary forces failed to find any gold. The only island in the Lesser Antilles that the Spaniards settled was the largest island of Trinidad, naming its capital St Joseph which was used as the 'jumping off' point to the mainland of South America. There is no record, however, of any local furniture from this period and Spain's involvement in the Lesser Antilles ended in 1797, with the capture of Trinidad by the British.

After a century of piracy and war against the Spanish the islands were settled in the sixteenth and seventeenth centuries by the competing European powers of France, England, Holland and Denmark. During this time the forests were cleared to plant cash crops such as indigo and cotton. The timber from these forests, such as rosewood, bulletwood, mahogany and other native woods, was sent back to the various Mother Countries to be used for ship building, houses and furniture. One evidence of this practice is a court cupboard in the Victoria and Albert Museum in London, made of bulletwood inlaid with satinwood which dates from the early 1600s. Also, in 1593 Sir Walter Raleigh presented Queen Elizabeth I with a table made from mahogany imported into England from the Antilles. This new wood, mahogany, became very popular in Europe. After the Antilles were settled and trade took off the cabinetmakers used this wood extensively from the early eighteenth century until today. The wood used in Denmark, France and England in the seventeenth century was mainly oak, imported from the Baltic, until the advent of mahogany. Walnut, from England and the Continent, and beech, one of the cheapest and most plentiful furniture woods from England, were also used.

When the joiners learned of the new wood called mahogany that grew in the West Indies, their interest was immediate. It had all the qualities of strength, hardness, straightness of grain and could be obtained in wide planks. They found it perfect for dining tables, the planks being wide enough to permit the making of the tops with three pieces or less, and it gave a perfect surface that took a fine polish. The import of mahogany from estates on British islands to England was tax free from 1722 onwards. The furniture of exotic West Indian woods was made in various European ports where factories were set up for the purpose of local and export trade. Some of the artisans were men who worked as carpenters on the ships of the 'Triangle Trade', between Europe, Africa, and the West Indies. When this trade slowed in the winter months, these carpenters would take up furniture-making in their respective ports, such as Nantes and Bordeaux in France, Liverpool and Bristol in England and Flensberg in Denmark.

It soon became obvious that European-made furniture could not stand up to the humidity and the termites. The Europeans used the expensive, imported woods such as mahogany and satinwood as a veneer on a lesser and cheaper base wood such as local pine and beech. This technique was workable for use in the Mother Countries, as termites and high humidity did not exist there. However, when this furniture was shipped back to the Antilles, it became apparent that termites or wood lice attacked or ate the soft secondary woods. In addition, the thin veneers soon warped in the high humidity. This changed the attitude towards the production of furniture made for export from the various Mother Countries. By the late eighteenth century you find pieces that were shipped from the Mother Countries, made from solid mahogany and in simpler design. Some of this furniture now had a secondary base of cedar (which is too bitter for the termites and had an attractive aromatic odour) and had thicker veneers. This became known as Port or Colonial Furniture and this technique was adapted and used in the Antilles.

With the discovery of the damage that termites and high humidity did to the pine carcasses and thin veneers, the Antilles craftsmen used different solutions to try to remedy this problem. They used hard woods and cedar for carcasses and thicker veneers on the traditional pine carcass. (Pine was the most available and inexpensive wood imported into the Antilles from the east coast of America and Canada. It was widely used for construction and furniture-making throughout the eighteenth, nineteenth and twentieth centuries.) The costly labour-intensive European inlay work and carving became less because the exotic woods used in the solid furniture increased the cost. This simpler and more elegant design, which depended on the figuration of the woods for their show, must have made the European image of the Antilles one of pastoral beauty and casual elegance. Also, the gilded bronze and brass handles, escutcheons, and mounts were replaced by designs made out of the various exotic woods.

One of the earliest mentions of West Indian Furniture was by Pierre La Batt, the French priest, on his travels to Martinique in 1694. He admired their furnishings and had a set of chairs made from rosewood. It is a pity he did not go into more explanation of the furniture he saw, but it would be easy to say that he did not have to pay as much for his solid rosewood chairs as he would have in France. (The same chairs in France would have had a soft wood substructure, such as pine or beech.) He would have slept in a native hammock or a rosewood or mahogany low post bed covered with a mosquito net that was hanging from the ceiling. His wardrobe, tables and other furniture could have been imported from France or have been made locally from solid woods in the image of the latest styles. He would have seen some carving but none of the elaborate baroque carving or inlay work of the seventeenth and early eighteenth century France.

Although European craftsmen came to the Antilles to train the island cabinetmakers, oral history supports the theory that the best island artisans were sent to their respective mother countries to be trained in their methods of furniture making. Further mention of this is made in the chapter on Danish Influences. By the early 1800s almost all the artisans working in the Antilles were locally born. The only insights we have of the eighteenth and nineteenth century artisan are a few cabinetmakers' labels that have survived (see Appendix 3).

The early colonists' needs were minimal: a chest, a table, a chair, some benches and the indigenous Indian hammock to sleep in. The pieces were simple and not made to last. Life was precarious and the idea was to make a fortune as quickly as possible, return home and live like a king. One of the earliest records we have of West Indian Furniture is of Jorgen Iversen, the first Governor of the Danish West Indies. He lived in two rooms at Fort Christian in St Thomas. In 1680, two inventories were drawn up stating that some of his furniture was locally made, and it would be easy to assume that the woods were native. Also the Danes and other early colonists used the native calabash or gourd and the coconut shells as utensils to serve and eat from. Eventually this changed and life became more settled. European wives demanded more gracious living and larger houses were built. More permanent and traditional European styled furniture was also in demand. As trade developed between the islands and also as ownership between them changed hands, there was a great mixing of furniture styles. The mixture of styles continued throughout this period, and it was not uncommon to see a Victorian table with Georgian and/or Empire features. The practice was not to be a slave to fashion, like the Mother Country, but to incorporate any new or popular elements into the standard design. After the emancipation of slavery in the 1830s in the British islands and the 1840s in the Danish and French islands, African West Indian carvers gave full reign to their interpretations of decorative motifs. They abandoned the European rigidity and conformity for a freer and less structured form of interpretation. Local details, such as palm fronds, flowers, leaves, animals, snakes and water motifs were adopted. These pieces dating from 1830–1860, are the most desirable. Another element that was introduced was caning for seats, and it was widely used because it allowed the circulation of air. The French and English introduced this form from their colonies and ports in India. Among the unique styles brought by the East Indians was their bangle which became the 'West Indian Bangle' and some of the filigree designs on the wood trim on the architecture and furniture of the nineteenth and early twentieth century, especially in Trinidad.

Armchair with caned seat.
Mahogany, Barbados, *circa* 1900.
35in. x 21in. x 19in.
The design of the back has been attributed to the 'Adinara' religion of the Ashanti people of Ghana, Africa. It represents the religious symbol 'Sankofa', a positive sign that teaches wisdom from the past to help build the future. It is used as an art form in jewellery, furniture, etc.

West Indian furniture has become rare and many pieces have disappeared during the tormented history of these islands. The majority of pre-1850 pieces were destroyed in fires which razed large parts of the towns and estate houses. Other factors were natural disasters such as hurricanes and earthquakes, and of course, revolutions. A major fire destroyed Bridgetown in Barbados, Charlotte Amalie of St Thomas had several disastrous fires in the early nineteenth century, and St Pierre, Martinique fell victim to a volcanic eruption. St Eustatius was destroyed by British Admiral Rodney for supporting and trading with the American rebels, and in 1843 an earthquake destroyed most of Pointe Pitre in Guadeloupe. All these contributing factors have depleted the older West Indian furniture, not to mention wood parasites. Wood parasites, white ants and termites, will eat all soft woods and the softer areas of hard woods. They will attack hard woods but soon turn back. This author has seen a large Bajan mahogany veneered sideboard, *circa* 1850, totally collapse because the pine carcass was eaten hollow by termites. Fortunately, a great deal of furniture was made from the harder woods like ironwood and have survived. Most important for the rarity of the furniture is the 'fickle finger of fashion' where pieces were abandoned, changed, or their wood reused for new furniture creating 'Evolutionary' pieces.

From the end of the Second World War through the 1940s and 1950s, elaborate carvings and lines gave way to a more austere type of furniture. These pieces lacked all individuality, were designed to be utilitarian and were mass-produced according to the latest modern designs. As a result, they do not have the character and romance found among the single and unique custom-made pieces of the past. Recently there has been a revival of furniture making using the past styles as the original antiques are becoming scarce. A trade in reproduction furniture has begun to blossom and, to the credit of many artisans, these pieces are so well designed and made that it is sometimes difficult to distinguish them from the antique.

Utensili de Garibi   *Migliavacca inc. 8*

THE INDIGENOUS FORMS AND FEATURES

Print showing indigenous Indians and the hammock they used.

Among their fine jewellery, textiles, wood and stone carvings, and their single log dugout canoes, the indigenous Indians of the Antilles have left two important furniture forms: the hammock and the ceremonial stool. When the Europeans first arrived they used the local furnishings like the Indians. The hammock was used for resting and relaxing during the day and as a bed for sleeping during the night. As time passed and the European planters became more affluent, they made low beds to sleep on, like they had in Europe, and used the hammock for relaxation. Eventually the hammock was reproduced into a more permanent piece of furniture in the form of the 'hammock chair', as it is known in Trinidad. The position of the sling of the hammock became important to the European, especially for relieving the swelling of his feet and for easy removal of his riding boots after a long day on horseback. This need prompted the invention of the hammock into a permanent piece of furniture called the 'Hammock' or 'Planter's' chair. This chair-form kept the same sling as the hammock but could now be moved in or out of doors as the person wished. The story that the European planters invented these chairs to remove their boots is secondary to the fact that the reclining position of the hammock lends itself to this usage.

The first instance of this innovation is recorded by the Spanish, but no hammock chairs from this period have survived. The earliest pieces on record are from the beginning of the nineteenth century, and were originally slung with canvas and had two arms extending forward to accommodate the sitter's feet. Sometimes these arms were in a fixed position and others folded back to take up less space. The fixed

positions are known as the 'male chair' and the fold back position as the 'female chair'. As time passed and these planters' chairs became a household fixture, they were made with upholstery or caning well into the twentieth century. Wherever the European met the indigenous hammock he seems to have made it into this chair. That is the reason this chair-form is found in Africa, India, the Philippines, the East and West Indies, Central and South America. Today this form is called the hammock or planter's chair, and also the 'Berbice' from a county in Guyana.

The other form comes from the Indian's ceremonial stool or 'Duho'. This low-slung stool with a tall curved back was made from precious woods, coral and stone, sometimes inlaid with gold, silver and shells. This form seems to have been adapted into a chair by the Spaniards in Campeche, Yucatan, a province of Mexico, and also in the Antilles where it is called a 'lolling chair'. Two chairs of this type are in the collection at Thomas Jefferson's 'Monticello' and are called 'Campeche' or Spanish chairs. The original stools were made of solid wood, but the European adaptations were usually slung with leather, fixed with brass nails and sometimes caned or upholstered.

There is a lot of debate as to the types of furniture developed especially for use in the islands by the Europeans. First, and most popular, is the rocking chair. This form came out of medieval Europe as the nurse's chair where a child could be held and rocked at the same time. In the late sixteenth–seventeenth century in England, rockers or gliders were attached to the child's cradle. This enabled the nanny or the mother to sit next to the rocking cradle and rock it by hand from side to side. Eventually these rockers or gliders were attached to the chair used by the nanny so as to facilitate the rocking of the child while being held by the nurse. The rocking chair soon left the nursery and became part of the bedroom furnishings. When it came west to Barbados (England's most important and prominent colony) it was used in public rooms and adapted to the tropics using caned seats and backs for cool air circulation. It then spread to the other British colonies in the West Indies and America. (It would be interesting to note here that Charleston South Carolina

Mahogany, caned Planters' Chairs, Barbados and St Thomas.
Male version, St Thomas, 1900.
Female version, Barbados, 1880.

Mahogany 'Lolling Chair'. Caned seat and back. Barbados, 1870.

41

was an extension of an over-populated Barbados. The single house plan in Charleston came from medieval England via Barbados.) Its development is claimed both by Barbados and America. What is certain is that it was developed for the tropics as its rocking movement and caned seat and back caught the breezes and, as Europe moved westward, Barbados was the first landfall before the American continent. The four-poster bed is another design from Europe that developed certain character changes for island use. It became higher to catch the breeze, usually the same height as the window-sills, with storage and extra sleeping space beneath. Mosquito netting and fine muslin was hung from the tester to protect the sleeper from disease-bearing mosquitoes and flying insects. The mattress was usually made from coarse linen and stuffed with coconut husks, dried grass, dried seaweed, and ends of cloth. Horsehair, which was available for upholstery, was sometimes used.

As rum was a by-product of the sugar industry it was sipped all day long, usually with water, orange or lime-juice, known as Planters Punch. This social custom of rum drinking spurred the invention of the bar in the West Indies as part of its furnishings, also known as the 'rum table'. These pieces of furniture were sometimes portable and could be moved around as needed. Indigenous to Barbados is the unique 'X-Frame Bar' with drawers in the top half of the X. The Virgin Islands produced what is called a 'cupping table' that looks like a cross between the traditional wash stand but without

Mahogany, French influence, 'Tall/High-Legged Console' or Bar. Trinidad, c.1880.

the hole for the wash bowl, and the sideboard with variations to the design. Here rum was also used from a crock with china cups instead of glasses. Curaçao (which was not a sugar or rum producing island) also produced a similar tall side table with a back splash called a 'water table'. The French islands also produced a tall table for the same usage which is called a 'high-legged console' or the French name 'consoles martiniquaises'. All these variations of the bar were taller than the other pieces of furniture in the room. Two more unique pieces of furniture produced in the Lesser Antilles come from Curaçao. They are the 'percha' and the 'lyre-shaped hall mirror'. The first piece of furniture resembles a wardrobe, without doors or back. It is open with a curtain to draw on the front with pegs on the back at the top to hang your coat. The second is a free-standing piece of furniture on a pedestal with a lyre-shaped frame holding a mirror with pegs on the frame for the hats. Another unique feature of Curaçao furniture are the corner pillars on some of their wardrobes. The pillars stand away from the corner at a forty-five degree angle and is a style inherited from the earlier Dutch interpretation of their 'Bombe Cornered Cabinets'.

Another design motif used is the snake or serpentine shape, sometimes in the form of a Baroque or Rococo 'S' scroll shape. The indigenous Taino, Carib and other Indian tribes together with many of the enslaved peoples from the west coast of Africa used the snake as a symbol of fertility in their religious ceremonies. This motif is found as part of the design on bed heads, chairs, tables, wash stands and other pieces of furniture used in the bedroom. Also the 'swan motif' was used in the French islands in the nineteenth century. It was used extensively after it was adopted by Empress Josephine of Martinique (wife of Napoleon I) as her personal motif in Malmaison, her home in France. Another piece of furniture found throughout the Lesser Antilles is 'the wagonette' also known as a food cart, food wagon and server. This piece of furniture was derived from the English Medieval 'Court Cupboard'. It was used in the Medieval Hall (this hall also served as a dining-room before being separated), and was usually of three rectangular shelves supported by four carved and/or turned corner posts which ended in turned or carved feet sometimes with castors. This form was sometimes made with drawers on the middle shelves and/or the bottom half enclosed

Mahogany Flower-Pot Stand with serpent carvings. St Thomas, *c*.1890.
Collection Corrine Lockhart.

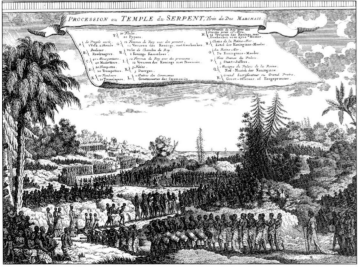

Africans in procession to the Serpent Temple for a ceremony.

Old print showing African Serpent Ceremony.

Mahogany
 Wagonette/Cart/Sideboard.
 Trinidad, *c*.1890.

with doors. The piece was usually surmounted by a carved back or crest and was made of the best mahogany with fine carvings, turnings and inlays. Other pieces were found made of pine, simply constructed and painted in suite with items such as stools, chairs, pie safes, tables and drying racks, for use in the kitchen, storeroom and pantry areas. This item of furniture was developed from a piece used as a dumb waiter that was kept in the kitchen/pantry area to be loaded with food and then wheeled into the dining-room and served from, to a permanent piece with a back to reside against a wall in the dining-room. It is now called a cart or side table. From Grenada there is a unique detail on the chaise-longue. The arm-rest or the foot end has incorporated into it a turned handle used for moving the piece around the room (see page 45). Barbados adopted a design from their locally made bread for their dining room chair back rail, of two inverted scrolls applied to each end of the rail. From the Virgin Islands, the turned spindled railing at the bottom of the four-poster beds seem to be an indigenous detail. After around 1830, palm fronds, flowers, leaves, shells, fern tendrils, herbs and other forms of local flora was used as decoration on all forms of furniture.

A piece of European furniture that developed a unique usage in the West Indies is the armoire or wardrobe. Firstly, an 'armoire' is the French name for a built-in shelf enclosure in the hall of a medieval fort or chateau. It was used to house pieces of armour and eventually this enclosure became separated from the panelled walls and became a free-standing piece of furniture. A similar story applies to the wardrobe in England. The central rooms of a fort or castle were called the ward, and it was in this area the robes of the church, state, and winter, etc. were kept. Out of this situation the name 'wardrobe' developed and was applied to a built-in section of the panelled great hall in medieval times. This wardrobe eventually became a free-standing piece of furniture. The West Indian usage of these case pieces was to lay flat on the shelves the ironed and pressed pieces of ladies' and gentlemen's outfits. The ladies' outfits were made up of several separate pieces of clothing such as camisoles, brassieres, crinolines, skirts, panties, blouses, shawls and jackets. The gentlemen also had several pieces that formed their outfits. All these pieces of clothing were placed on top of each other in rows with covered bricks pressing them flat. These bricks were building bricks that were covered with several layers of cotton or linen and were placed upon the clothing to keep them flat or pressed. This is the reason why wardrobes and armoires are called 'presses' in the Lesser Antilles. These presses came in three different sizes depending on the owners' needs. A smaller style of this press was also used in the dining-rooms for linens and was called a parlour or linen press. Another interesting piece of furniture is the single door 'hanging press'. This style developed simultaneously throughout the world with the invention and manufacture of the hook and eye in the 1850s and the zipper in the 1890s. These inventions gave the designer a great device to hold together in one piece a lady's or a gentleman's outfit. This became very popular and the hanging press came into being. Now the entire outfit would be hung on a peg and stay somewhat pressed which eventually resulted in the invention of the hanger. The single door hanging presses were made for hanging, but a two door press with half hanging and half shelved became the most popular form in the twentieth century.

The popular pastime of card playing and gambling produced one of the most recognized forms in the Antilles, the card table. The most popular version of the cards/games table was the felt lined folding table with a swivel top to open and close, exposing a well to hold the cards and chips. Also used for these games was the folding tea table where no felt was included but a sheet of it used over the playing area. These tea/card/dining tables were called 'universal tables'.

Detail of the back handle on a mahogany and cane Chaise-Longue from Grenada, c.1870. This arm detail, used to move the Chaise, is indigenous to that island.

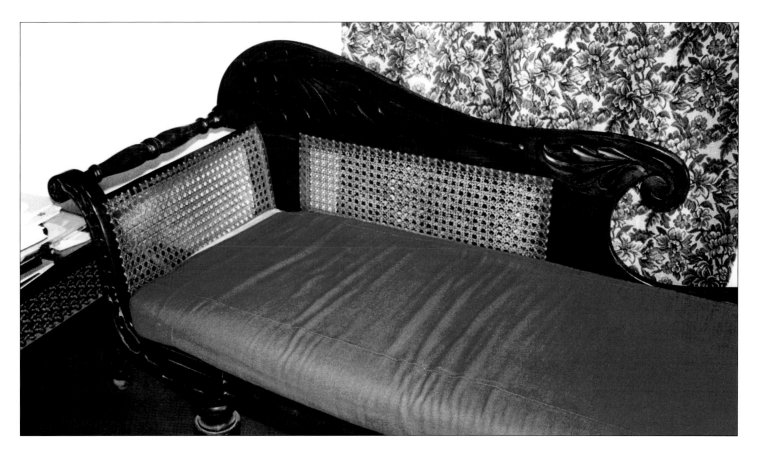

Details of Indigenous Features on Antilles Furniture

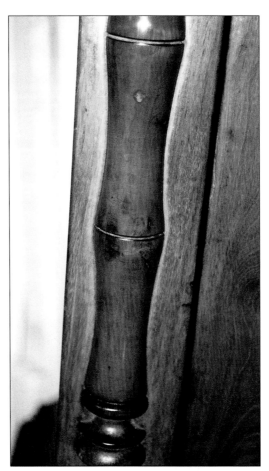

Detail on a sofa table showing an example of the toe in the form of a Sand Box wood fruit.

Lamination or applying one or more layers of wood together for extra thickness to carve a protruding detail (sometimes called a 'cheek') is most often seen on bed-posts, legs and columns of furniture made in Curaçao. The photograph shows a detail of a bed-post from Curaçao with an applied lamination which is then carved with a reeded design.

Detail of a bamboo design on an armoire from Curaçao.

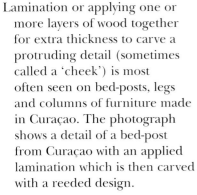

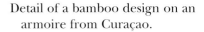

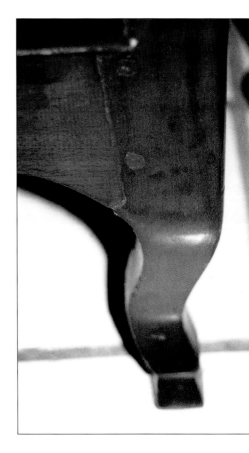

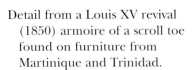

Detail from a Louis XV revival (1850) armoire of a scroll toe found on furniture from Martinique and Trinidad.

This hoof toe on the same style armoire as the one on the left is only found on furniture from St Thomas and may even be an import from New Orleans.

Spurred sabre leg motif.

Swan foot motif.

The pineapple motif on left, Barbados table, *c*.1800 and right St. Croix bed, *c*.1830.

The palm leaf frond motif.

THE AMERICAN INFLUENCE

The thirteen colonies of America produced fine furniture of English design, which continued after independence from England in 1776. Before 1776 England only allowed trade between the British colonies in the Antilles, free-ports, and the Americas. Colonial and independent America had, and still has, a great influence on the Lesser Antilles. Trade was booming between the British Americas and the West Indies, and after the War of Independence America acquired more trading partners in the French Antilles. The result of the French aiding America against the British was a turning point for furniture design motifs in America and the Antilles. American/French Antillean trade and influence was enhanced and the English/American style had some influences in the French Antilles. Motifs of the 'New England' style were adapted for the products of the French islands and soon this helped in creating the French-Creole style. Federal influences, especially on the cornices and motifs on the island armoires, cabinets and tables helped in producing an interesting hybrid.

As a result of the export trade, many American cabinetmakers took special orders for the West Indies. Some of these cabinetmakers are recorded, such as:

Joseph B. Barry, worked in Philadelphia from 1794–1844.
William Camp, worked in Baltimore from 1802–1823.
Charles Christian, worked in New York from 1810–1815.
Job Clark, worked in Newport from 1751–1774.
Duncan Phyfe, worked in New York from 1795–1847.

In the nineteenth century many cabinetmakers moved to the Antilles to set up shop. One known artisan was Robert Saw, who was active on Front and Second Streets in Philadelphia from 1796–1833 when he moved to Havana, Cuba. The account book of Robert Jenkins Jnr., (Rhode Island Historical Society, Providence) records that on 20th February 1752, cabinetmaker Silas Cook of Newport transported on the ship *Mary Ann* to the West Indies '12 frames for chairs, 2 frames for arm chairs and 3 backgammon tables valued at 150 pounds.' It would appear that the chair frames would be upholstered or caned in the Antilles. Another record from the French émigré cabinetmaker Honoré Lannuier who worked in New York from 1805–1890 is a listing from his inventory, 'Furniture sent to the West Indies, $534.00.'

During the early nineteenth century and after the 1812 War, French Empire and English Regency styles influenced American furniture. As America became more of an international importer and exporter, styles from around the world had their influences. Many of the nineteenth century designers in America were from Paris, such as Charles Honoré Lannuier and Anthony Quervelle who were responsible for the strong French influence in American designs. American designers like Joseph Meeks and Sons of New York, Charles H. White and Joseph Barry of Philadelphia, introduced the Egyptian and Gothic styles to American Furniture. Coherence in American design was gradually lost until the regulating influence of the 1876 Philadelphia Centennial Exposition. It was during the nineteenth century that the pineapple and lyre motifs became more popular in the Antilles through American designs and influences.

The century, which began with the careful designs of the Federal Period, soon gave way to a confusion and search for new ideas which was to continue with many revival styles, then fashionable in Europe, until the arrival of the Arts and Crafts movement. The English designer Charles Eastlake's book, 'Hints on Household Taste' was adopted by America and his designs became known as 'Eastlake Style'. This furniture book was widely available and a great influence in the Antilles, especially the Dutch Islands. These designs along with the Shaker-style influences spread throughout the Antilles, where its clean lines were easily mass-produced. By the beginning of the twentieth century, William Morris, Frank Lloyd Wright, and Gustav Stickley were influencing most of the new furniture designs in America and beyond. Their 'Honest' styles and construction were very popular and practical for craftsmen in the Antilles as their production was easier and faster. Their furniture design books and catalogues also had a wide influence in the Antilles, where many furniture shops carried American and locally made pieces. These American mass-produced pieces together with iron and brass beds, furniture and accessories, with all the other European imports soon left the Antillean Artisan on the sidelines to do custom, reproduction and restoration work.

Mahogany universal folding table with shaped top, carved, turned legs and beaded decoration on the apron with fine figured woods. There is a definite American Federal influence on this table. Trinidad, c.1830.

One of a pair of rocking chairs made from 'Cordia Wood' (*cordia Gerascanthoides* H.B.K.). There is a distinct American Eastlake influence on this chair with the spindled decoration. Barbados, c.1900.

THE BRITISH-ENGLISH INFLUENCE

Engand soon challenged Spain's hold on the Lesser Antilles, firstly, by pirating and privateering, and after many claims and failed settlements on Saint Lucia (1605), Barbados (1615), and Tobago (1623), the English finally settled on Saint Kitts in 1623. In 1624, Barbados, the most windward of the Antilles, became their main port and emporium to America. Then they settled Barbuda in 1627, Antigua in 1632, Anguilla in 1650 and Tortola in 1666. No furniture of the seventeenth century British West Indies has survived and the earliest known pieces date from around 1740. These pieces were totally influenced by English designs. Thomas Chippendale, Thomas Sheraton, George Hepplewhite and Thomas Hope were leading furniture designers in the eighteenth and nineteenth century in England. They published design books that were used in the colonies. One of the first furniture entrepreneurs was Thomas Chippendale of London. He published his 'Gentlemen and Cabinetmaker's Director' in 1754 which was bought by furniture artisans, suppliers and plantation owners who had their local craftsmen execute the designs. This book was used throughout the British West Indies and also found its way to the other islands. Chippendale was one of the most significant furniture designers and makers in the school of classical furniture and his fame spread throughout Europe and the colonies.

These designers influenced the British West Indies and their local products are considered some of the finest furniture (sometimes indistinguishable from their English counterparts and on a par with American examples) made in the Lesser Antilles. The development of the English style in Barbados influenced all the other British posessions, including the American colonies. It is believed the same way that Barbados influenced the development of the Carolinas, especially the architecture of Charleston, so it was with the furniture styles. It must be remembered that before there was an American Chippendale, Sheraton, Hepplewhite or Regency style, these styles had already been developed in Barbados. Barbados is also pre-eminent in the Americas for the beauty and age of its country houses. There are four Jacobean houses (1560–1620) in the western hemisphere, three of them in Barbados and the other in Virginia in the American colony. In 1700, Pierre Labat the French cleric travelling through the Antilles described the interior of the houses in Barbados, writing, ' ...the opulence and good taste of the inhabitants may be remarked in their furniture which is magnificent and in their silver, which they have in considerable quantities.'

In 1778, after France with its ally, the newly independent United States of America declared war on Britain, the latter decided to garrison Barbados permanently as the headquarters of the Leeward and Windward islands, to protect their interest in the Caribbean. This caused a large influx of Army personnel, their families and dependants, into the Bajan society, causing a stir and influencing furniture styles. With all this, came the demand for 'Campaign Furniture' and other furnishings. Furniture made for military campaigns and used mostly by the officers, collapsed, folded, unscrewed and divided for easy transportation. It included chairs, desks, lap

INTERIOR.
View of the drawing-room with Mahogany double-ended caned sofa from Barbados, *circa* 1870. Collection: Adrian Camps-Campins.

INTERIOR.
View of the drawing room with late nineteenth century piano, English, *circa* 1880. Collection: Adrian Camps-Campins

desks, beds, chests, cellarets and boxes. The construction of all these pieces had necessary brass boundings for extra strength. All the joints, and especially the corners were brass protected. The handles were flush with the pulls recessed, and they sometimes had an inlaid shield or square for a coat of arms. It was not long before the 'campaign style' was popular, leading to many pieces being made for private purchase. These pieces are easily identified, as they do not collapse or come apart. This 'campaign style' with its straight lines and brass decorations remained one of the forms produced in Barbados throughout the 18th and 19th centuries, especially the folding chair. After all threats were gone Britain removed the last of her troops in Barbados in 1905 and they were replaced by a battalion of the 1st West Indian Regiment.

After the 1838 hurricane in Barbados, the furniture cottage craft was expanded and upgraded for exportation. Barbados exported furniture during the eighteenth and nineteenth century to the other British colonies including America, especially Charleston. (The colony of Carolina with its city of Charleston, was born of the charter given by Charles II to his supporters in England and Barbados. The eight loyalists known as 'The Lords proprietors of Carolina', together with the overflow of colonists in Barbados moved and established Charleston on the Ashley (named after a Bajan planter) River in 1663. It had six out of ten parishes named after the Barbados model, and Barbados also exported its unique medieval single house design to Charleston.) A lot of furniture from England's ports (see chapter on port furniture) were also imported into the British West Indies and were used as models by the local artisans. This continued throughout the eighteenth, nineteenth and twentieth centuries. In the beginning the furniture was made exactly as the British product, using a carcass of imported inexpensive woods such as pine, with veneers and inlays of mahogany, satin-wood, etc. Barbados imported its mahogany and other exotic woods from Honduras and Jamaica, until it planted its own mahogany trees in the 1780s. (In the seventeenth century the island was one of the first to level the forests and plant sugar throughout.)

By the 1820s Barbados produced enough furniture to export fully to the other islands and to the free-ports, and throughout the British West Indies large stores sold local, British, and Bajan furniture. After Spanish Trinidad became British in 1797, it started to import furniture from Barbados on a large scale. The artisan in Trinidad produced furniture in the French design (from the French émigré population) and by 1800 the English in Trinidad were producing their own designs. Dominica, St Vincent, St Lucia and Grenada produced a hybrid style coming from their French/English occupations and influences. Montserrat, St Kitts, Tortola and Antigua produced English-style furniture for local consumption. As an example, in British Trinidad the firm of Davidson and Todd were furniture makers and sellers. This establishment was founded in the 1850s by James Todd which employed furniture makers, but sadly none of their names are known. Their craftsmanship was some of the best in the West Indies and is mentioned in the 'Commercial Port of Spain' conducted by Alistair McMillen in 1905. It says the big furniture department in 'The Trinidad Arcade' is an object lesson in what can be accomplished by skill, experience, and conscientious effort. The beautiful native woods of the colonies are here worked into bedroom suites, dining-room suites and drawing-room suites. The roll-top desk, cabinets, etc., cannot fail to elicit the praise of the most authoritative exponents of the trade in Great Britain and it is not surprising to learn that Messrs Davidson and Todd obtained the first prize for their work at the Trinidad Exhibition in 1901. The designs are correct to the

Pie/Food Safe with Bread Box
  Top.
  Saman wood, copper netting.
  Made in Trinidad, *c.* 1920.
  59in. x 36in. x 18in.

minutest detail, the woods are perfectly prepared, the workmanship the most skilled obtainable, the finish superlatively produced and nothing is left undone to maintain the high reputation that has been gained in this direction.

Queen Victoria's reign (1834–1901) produced a century of high growth and the rise of a large middle class. This new clientele was only too happy to have styles from the past and the revivals took place. The main styles of the Victorian period are: the classical Greek and Roman styles, Louis XIV mixed with Rococo, Elizabethan mixed with Jacobean and Gothic and the influences of all the past designers of the eighteenth century. Classical styles were based on the Regency and Empire styles from the 1820s, their designs becoming more coarsened and the term sub-classical has been applied to these pieces. In the British Antilles this style has been called 'late Regency' or 'William IV'. The revival of Louis XV or the Rococo style of the eighteenth century was very popular and widely applied to seating accommodations. Very florid, scrolled and plant designs were also used on drawing-room furniture and upholstery and caning was widely used on these pieces. The English Victorian revival designs were a great influence all over Europe, hence the spread of this influence to all the Lesser Antilles. In Trinidad some of the finest furniture in the Lesser Antilles was produced during the Edwardian Revival Period (1900–1925). Fine furniture was produced until the Second World War when the demand for quick comfort by a larger clientele turned to machine made and imported products. Furniture making is still a profitable business, but mostly these artisans do repair and restoration work and custom pieces. The British West Indies went through the stylistic customs of England with the nineteenth century revivals, the Art Nouveau, Arts and Crafts, and the Art Deco Periods producing some of the finest pieces in these styles.

THE DANISH INFLUENCE

Small cabinet with glass doors.
Mahogany, St Thomas, U.S. V.I.
Circa 1910.
Attributed to Fernando Essanason,
37½ in. x 23in. x 18in.

Armchair with caned back and seat.
Mahogany, Louis XIV Revival.
St Thomas, U.S. V.I. *Circa* 1910.
Attributed to Fernando
Essanason, 43in. x 21in. x 19in.

The Danish West Indian and Guinea Company of Denmark, settled St Thomas in 1665, St John in 1717 and St Croix in 1733. The Dutch and British initially settled St Croix and the French held it from 1650–1733. There seems to be little or no surviving furniture or influences from these earlier settlements except for some Great Houses and forts on St Croix and St Thomas. The major influence on the architecture and furniture design that is found is from its period of Danish occupation which was until 1917 when the United States of America purchased the islands, to protect the Caribbean sea lanes during the First World War.

Danish furniture styles in the Lesser Antilles produced some interesting hybrid forms. English influence on Danish furniture is evident stemming from the export of timber from Norway (part of Denmark at the time) to England. Dutch influences were also taken up due to political and commercial ties. Members of the Copenhagen Guild produced special orders with the German influence, as

one member Mathias Ortmann (*circa* 1760) is well known by his labelled pieces. Neo-classicism was introduced to Denmark in 1757 by the French architect Nicolas Jardin who trained Danish furniture designer D. F. Harsdorff (1735–99). In 1750 the Academy of Copenhagen was set up with the furniture off-shoot the *Kongelige Meubel Magazin* (Royal Furniture Emporium) being established in 1779. Its director Carsten Ankar was an enthusiast for English styles (partly due to the Queen who was the sister of the English King George III and married to Denmark's Christian VII, 1766–1808). Ankar sent Danish craftsmen to England to improve their skills. Jens Brotterup was such a craftsman who, on his return to Copenhagen, taught his newly learned skills to the Danish artisans. This resulted in the production of a lot of English influenced furniture, which was also felt at the port of Flensberg where the furniture for the Antilles was produced.

Another furniture designer of the 'second phase neo-classicism' was Nikolai A. Bildgaard (1743–1809), and a post-empire fashion for mahogany furniture was spread throughout Scandinavia by Gustav Hetsch who died in 1857. It was during this period of the nineteenth century that many artisans from the Danish West Indies (e.g. Charles MacFarland) went to Denmark to further their training and returned to the islands to spread their knowledge. It was also during this period that this Danish furniture product with its Dutch, German and English influences was introduced and spread throughout the Danish West Indies. The German influence became part of the design element when Flensberg was absorbed into Germany after 1850 (see chapter on Port Furniture). The end product in the colonies was a distinctive design that is not so easily recognizable. After the late Empire Period, *circa* 1840–50, it seems all the furniture produced in the Danish West Indies followed the forms of nineteenth century Europe using local design elements and motifs well into the first half of the twentieth century.

Cabinet
Mahogany, Fernando Essanason.
Danish West Indies. *Circa* 1900.
Collection: Corrine Lockhart.

THE DUTCH INFLUENCE

The Dutch came to the Antilles in the early 1600s to set up centres to promote their slave trading. The three islands of Curaçao, Aruba and Bonaire were central to the shipping lanes of the Spanish Empire builders. The Dutch West India Company settled these islands in 1642, while other Dutch settled St Maarten in 1620 to protect their shipping. They also settled St Eustatius in 1636, so by 1640 the Dutch were firmly established in the Lesser Antilles to continue their naval trade. They built in their typical Dutch architectural style which has survived and the outstanding town of Willemstad in Curaçao is now a World Heritage Site. Their typical curvilinear gables and dormer decorations of the 1700s, mixed with the bright Caribbean colours makes this town an architectural gem.

The Netherland Antilles developed differently from the other Lesser Antilles as they had no forests. The British and French Islands had great resources of mahogany and other hard woods. The British islands sent mahogany to England and returned a finished furniture product to their islands, as did the Danes in their islands. The Dutch Islands imported hardwoods from their South American colony of Surinam. Many traders and civil servants brought furniture with them which were used as models that had an effect on the local production and market. The furniture of Curaçao was of great beauty and outstanding craftsmanship, but little is left from the seventeenth and eighteenth century. At first some furniture and design books were brought over from Holland, but as time passed the colonists produced many indigenous and fine pieces. This furniture was shipped to all the free-ports in the Lesser Antilles (St Thomas, St Eustatius, St Barthelemy to name a few), and Venezuela in South America.

The advent of Dutch design in Europe followed the crowning of Dutchman William III of Orange in England to support the Protestant cause. Furniture designer Daniel Marot followed William III to England where he worked as a court designer and returned to Holland in 1698. The indigenous Dutch form gave England its two-piece chest on chest or tallboy. These chests had either all drawers or cupboards and drawers and were in two parts. The demand for English- and French-style furniture became so great in Holland in the 1760s, that the local production became threatened. In 1771, all imports were banned except for pieces at their annual furniture shows. The Amsterdam Guild of St Joseph marked their pieces with the initials J.G. (for Joseph's Guild) to distinguish the Dutch pieces from foreign imports. Even with this measure Dutch furniture continued to be influenced by French and English styles. In 1795, Capel Breytspraak became master and produced styles with detailing and turns from the Dutch seventeenth century. Another cabinetmaker G. Nurdanus supplied mahogany pieces at the Hague in 1818, all in a simple version of the English Regency Style.

Furniture production in Curaçao was prolific with many artisans producing

Renaissance revival. Secretaire by Thomas Chapman of Curaçao. Mahogany with cordia panel and inlays, c.1900

Mahogany serpentine-shaped side table with exaggerated cabriole legs, draped carvings on knees and applied rondels on the shaped apron. There is not a straight line on this piece of furniture. Dutch Curaçao, *c.*1875.

MAKER'S LABEL.
Depiction of Maker's Label on Armoire.

ARMOIRE 1890–1920.
Curaçao-Dutch Influence.
Ht.90" W.60" D.25"
This armoire is made of Mahogany with a Pine sub-structure. The two doors have bevelled mirrored insets, with split balusters on both sides and in the middle of the doors, in a turned, reeded and bamboo design. There are two drawers on the bottom, sitting on a shaped platform with porcelain castors. The top has a shaped, carved and engraved design with a moulded crown. This piece has five maker's labels inside. The label is in three languages: Dutch?, Spanish?, or Pempermento, which is the local dialect.

fine furniture in the nineteenth century. Their production was marked by their economic ups and downs and some of the finest furniture was made during the first quarter of the twentieth century. About 1850, the American mass-production of furniture started to have an influence on the Antilles. As a result, in Curaçao the Dutch styles were being replaced by American influences affecting the design of its local production. There was a great influence by the American Eastlake designs which was spread by catalogues at this time. Stylistic motifs and forms in the Dutch West Indies also went through the Art Nouveau and Art Deco periods producing some of the finest pieces in the Lesser Antilles. After the Second World War, furniture started to be produced by machinery and the artisans were sidelined to the restoration of old pieces and customer orders.

THE FRENCH INFLUENCE

French influence. Screen –
   Louis XV-style.
   Mahogany, *circa* 1880.
   Trinidad.

The French were one of the first (with the English) to come to the Lesser Antilles after the Spanish and challenged their exclusive claims. They became pirates and buccaneers, supported by their King, attacking the Spanish treasure fleets and finally settled on Tortuga, in the late 1500s, which became their base to keep up the pressure on the Spaniards. The Spanish chased them from Tortuga in the 1630s, and in the 1640s the French from St Kitts (which they had shared with the English since 1625) resettled Tortuga. Martinique and Guadeloupe were settled in 1635. The French were serious settlers, many of them second sons from aristocratic families, who paid the Compagnie des Iles d'Amérique for their sea voyage. In the 1640s the French Governor of the Antilles, Chevalier Phillipe de Longvillers de Poincy, built the grandest palace in the Lesser Antilles in St. Kitts. Only some of the out-buildings and foundations remain. All the furniture for this palace was believed to have come from France.

This new tendency to import furniture from France in the seventeenth century could have created a difficult risk and competition for a new born artisan in the French Antilles. A royal regulation was published towards a long term economy for the islands which forbade any introduction of furniture built in France, or in Europe. The only ones exempted from this decision were the ship captains. The regulation also stated that all furniture was to be built on the islands and that the time for apprenticeship to join the Guilds in France would be shortened from three to two years. The artisans could go to the Antilles with the understanding that they could return to Paris and start their own business, after this two year apprentice. This was a great opportunity for the craftsmen as the strict rules of the Furniture Guilds and Corporations of Paris made it almost impossible for an artisan from outside of Paris to establish himself there.

Many artisans came to the Antilles with the insurance that the latest furniture design books would be carried and provided by the ship captains. These French provincial artisans quickly established themselves and soon started to charge unbearable prices for their products, so the planters, who already had talented African and European carpenters on their plantations, were soon making furniture that was affordable and eventually squeezed out the over-pricing. These local artisans soon hired themselves out to other plantations and many of the enslaved made enough money to buy their freedom. The earlier pieces made by the

apprentices from France (most returned) were used widely as models by these local craftsmen, and quite a few of these pieces have survived. Also the occupation of Martinique, 1794-1802 and 1809-1815, and Guadeloupe in 1794 by the British, brought about much cultural exchange with nearby Barbados.

With this unique occurrence in the French Antilles the furniture in these islands soon started to take on a singular 'creole style' and the situation made it easy for the artisan to be influenced from the outside. Barbados exported English furniture design books and locally made furniture to Martinique in the eighteenth and nineteenth centuries. In 1791, The Paris Furniture Guilds with their restrictive codes, were swept away with The French Revolution. By then, the mixture of French and English styles in Martinique (the two leading styles in Europe) produced a 'Creole Style' in the *oeuvre* of Martiniquan Furniture. (The strongest Barbadian/English influence can be seen in their beds and seating furniture.) With France's involvement in the American Revolution the French Antilles had a large trade with the east coast of America. This English/Barbadian/American influence on the style of furniture in the islands is recognizable especially in the pieces of the nineteenth century.

These laws did not apply to the French émigrés from the wars, pestilence and revolutions from the French Antilles, who resettled in Trinidad and some of the other English islands during the second half of the eighteenth century. In 1783, Trinidad had a population of 731 and by 1809 it was in excess of 30,000. This was due largely to French Antillean resettlement. Some of the most outstanding furniture of French styles was produced in Trinidad where the French were the largest dominant political/cultural force in the Spanish Colony. Some of the finest Louis XV, XVI and Empire styled furniture was produced here during the eighteenth and nineteenth centuries. Even after the British took Trinidad from the Spanish in 1797, the French continued making furniture in the French Style alongside the British.

French furniture influences and forms in the Antilles came from several designers in Paris. The baroque designs of the seventeenth century, the Régence, the Rococo of the eighteenth century and the neo-classical of the late eighteenth and early

French influence. Keyhole-covers made from wood instead of metal.

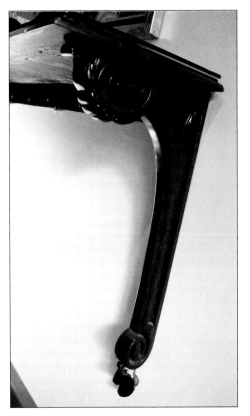

French influence. Louis XV-style scroll and leaf detail on shelf bracket.
Mahogany, Trinidad. 1860.

nineteenth century were adapted and reworked by the artisans of the French Antilles. The baroque designers were Jean le Pautre (1618-82), Jean Berian (1637-1711) and André Charles Boulle (1642-1732) who were all 'Maître-Ebenistes' or head cabinet designers and makers to the court. The Compagnie des Indes founded in 1664 imported design elements from India and China which influenced designs in France, which in turn influenced designs in the Antilles. In the eighteenth century we have designer Charles Cressent (1685-1758), and Bernard II van Risenbursh (1700-65), who was famous for the Rococo design, (a lighter form of the baroque designs) which had 'S' and 'C' scrolls and shell and flower motifs. The neo-classical (with its straighter lines, its design elements coming from the discovery of the ancient Roman cities of Pompeii and Herculaneum) was made famous by designers Adam Weisweiler (1750-1810) and J. H. Reisener during the last years of the eighteenth century. The French Revolution (1789-1793) introduced simpler lines with less decoration.

In France, after being released from prison in 1795, Josephine de Beauharnais of Martinique (future wife of Napoleon Bonaparte) purchased Chantereine, a house she restored and furnished with pieces from the Antilles. Frédéric Masson, the French author writes, '…what pretty furniture she had, a mahogany dressing table, a writing table of Guadeloupe walnut, an octagonal yellow wood centre table, and a secretary of yellow wood framed with redwood with a mirror and a marble top'. Napoleon's conquest of Egypt in 1798 introduced Egyptian motifs into the new French Empire Style. Its simpler lines were quickly adopted in France and its colonies (as can be seen in the fine pieces made in French Trinidad). The foremost designers of the Empire Style were Charles Percier (1764-1838) and Pierre Fontaine (1762-1853) who published in 1801 'Recueil des Décorations Intérieurs' which was used in the Antilles, and Henri Jacob (1763-1824). After the Battle of Waterloo in 1815 and the return of the House of Bourbon to the throne, furniture design became simpler and the rest of the nineteenth century saw the revivals of the Medieval, Baroque, Régence, Rococo, Neo-classical and Empire styles until the late nineteenth century with the event of machine-made furniture. The need for large amounts of cheap serviceable furniture was in big demand, as the population of France and the Antilles had become much larger. The industrial age of steel driven saws and veneer knives was fully used to fill this demand. The nineteenth century growth of the middle class and more opportunity for everyone resulted in many more households with larger families.

The 1800s saw the revival of all the former styles. Nineteenth century individuals wanted styles of their past to celebrate their new-found riches. Many of the styles they sought to improve upon: a Renaissance theme would quickly be adapted to the new needs, a Louis XIII style would be resized to the new interiors, baroque details would be on a transitional piece with a Louis XV base. This new movement and mixing of styles was totally accepted by the island artisans and clients. This eclecticism was born and lasted until the 1920s. Together with all of this and the Anglomania of the Louis-Philippe Period, Great Britain was able to influence France and the Antilles and also brought a love for the exotic styles of the East. The reaction by some designers against this repetition saw the brief but artistic period of Art Nouveau (1890-1914) and also designs of the Art Deco (1920-1940) Movement which flowered between the two World Wars. There was not a sharp change from the eclectic to the natural forms of Art Nouveau. The change started in the 1870s with the introduction of plant forms. These naturalistic motifs and sinuous plant forms began to define the forms of the furniture rather than being just decorative. The designs of the furniture makers Louis Majorelle and Alexander Charpentier soon made their way into the workshops and studios of the Antilles, producing a pleasing combination of mahogany in many original plant form designs. Tables were produced with supports in the style of a twisting vine and the top a large lily leaf. A lot of this Art Nouveau furniture was produced in the Antilles, but goes largely unrecognized.

Ultimately it was the First World War and its aftermath that brought together all the diverse elements and produced an international style. During the 1930s European furniture was more advanced in design than before and the Scandinavian designers were copied throughout Europe, America and the Antilles. It was simple in appearance, well made from quality materials and could be sold through catalogues or directly customer-ordered. In 1925 there was a great show of furniture and other art at the Paris International Exhibition. From this came the style popularly known as 'Art Moderne' or 'Art Deco' which applied to designs, inspired by the lines of machinery, industry and speed. This exhibition, despite its title, was mostly a French affair showing furniture designs by Ruhlman, Dunard, Follot and others. This Art Deco style became universal, it was very popular in the Antilles and its simple lines even enable it to be placed in today's modern interiors. Furniture produced by industrial factories started in the Lesser Antilles in the second quarter of the twentieth century. This caused the demise of the hand-crafted product and the only furniture made by the craftsmen were custom orders, reproduction and restoration work.

The artisans of the French Antilles being freed from any stylistic or governmental restrictions produced fine unique furniture, being very adventurous with different and unusual woods. Precious woods such as courbaril, purple heart, satinwood and roble wood were used in solid form for cabinets, beds, armoires, etc.

French influence. Drawing of Sleigh Bed.
Mahogany, Martinique, *circa* 1870.
Drawing by Gary Palmatier.

THE SPANISH INFLUENCE

When Christopher Columbus came upon the Lesser Antilles in the 1490s on his quest to find the Orient, he claimed them for his sponsors the King and Queen of Spain. The Spaniards were only interested in gold, therefore these islands having no gold, remained unoccupied. Only Trinidad the largest of the Lesser Antilles was occupied as an outpost or stepping stone to South America. Soon Spain's European rivals were fighting each other for these unoccupied islands. During the sixteenth, seventeenth and eighteenth centuries they were taken and retaken by Britain, Holland, France and Denmark until the last Spanish territory of Trinidad, in the Lesser Antilles, was conquered by the British in 1797. No furniture of Spanish origin or influence seems to have survived in the Lesser Antilles and the 'Spanish Chair', 'leather Spanish Chair', and the 'Spanish leg Chair' that we read in inventories of Trinidad and Curaçao would have been imported from Venezuela or Colombia or possibly locally made. The adaptation of the Indian hammock to a stationary piece of furniture known as the hammock or planter's chair, and the lolling or 'campeche' chair, based on the Indian ceremonial stool are attributed to the Spaniards. Only remnants of forts, buildings, foundations, churches and names remain to remind us of Spain's presence in the Lesser Antilles.

Spanish influence. Trinidad. Mahogany table with metal strengthener, *circa* 1770.

THE SWEDISH INFLUENCE

Swedish influence in the Lesser Antilles was fleeting. After France exchanged the island of St Barthelemy in 1784 for trading rights in Sweden, the Swedes turned the island into a free-port. As a free-port, pieces of furniture from England, America, France, Sweden and the exporting islands of the Antilles would have been imported and sold from this one small island throughout the Antilles, during its periods of varied ownerships. The Swedes returned the island to France in 1879 and their locally made pieces of furniture were limited. Swedish neo-classical style was the most popular design and all the pieces known are with simple straight lines and tapered legs. Their decoration depended on the figuration and line of the mahogany, sometimes with a string inlay of satinwood. Several tables with inlaid chessboards have survived from the nineteenth century. Very little furniture from the eighteenth and the nineteenth centuries has survived after Mother Nature's hurricanes and earthquakes ravaged the island several times.

Swedish influence.
  Mahogany universal table 'neo-classical' style. Turned legs, inlaid centre plaque on apron, gate-leg, *c.*1800.

Swedish influence.
  Games table with painted chessboard top. 'Bobbin' turned legs, stretcher and toes, *c.*1890.

PORT FURNITURE

I.   Timber goes to factory in port, from the islands.

II. Furniture made in factory and shipped back to islands, hence 'port furniture'.

III. European and African artisans use the furniture as models, to produce for local consumption.

IV. Best African apprentices are sent to the same port factories, in the mother countries, for further and final training.

V.   Therefore, the continuation of the same techniques are learned and carried forward, making the separation of port and locally made furniture a difficult one.

The European settlers in the Lesser Antilles found the islands covered with virgin forests of mahogany, cedar, purple heart, crapaud, ebony and a host of new and unusual hard woods. Many of these forests were cleared, especially on level land, to plant cash crops such as indigo and tobacco with products like maize and cassava for local consumption and large stretches of land were used for horse and cattle ranching. The large logs of these trees were shipped back to their respective mother countries where they were used for buildings and furniture. Some of the furniture was produced especially to be shipped back to the islands and in most cases was made to be collapsible. Armoires were made to be assembled without the use of screws or nails, table-tops and legs unscrewed and unmounted parts were sent to be fitted together and finished in the islands. All this was to save as much room as possible in the holds of the cargo ships, (some pieces became one quarter of their size after collapsing) as this furniture was also used as ballast as well as future examples for the local artisans.

The 'Triangle Trade' of the Atlantic slowed and sometimes stopped during the winter months and the craftsmen of these ships found employment in the furniture factories in their respective ports. A substantial number of pieces were sold locally and the rest shipped to the islands in the Antilles and the different free-ports. In England, ports such as Liverpool, Bristol and London had many of these factories. One of the well-known furniture makers in England that supplied the British West Indies was Gillows of Lancaster, founded by Robert Gillow Senior in about 1728 or 1729. It grew and prospered and the firm opened a premises in London from where furniture was also shipped. By 1800, the firm had expanded, exporting considerable amounts of furniture to the West Indies. They seem to be the only English firm to adopt the French custom of signing or stamping their furniture. Between 1781 and 1813 one hundred and eighty-three ships sailed from the port of Lancaster of which a small number were carrying furniture for the firm of Worswick and Allman on the island of St Kitts. Richard and Robert Gillow were the uncles of Thomas Worswick (born 1760), the merchant on St Kitts. He regularly purchased furniture from his uncles' firm and sold it throughout the Antilles. The rare and tropical hardwoods were used as veneers and inlay on a carcass of less expensive soft wood and this port furniture was first used as models by the European and African craftsmen in the islands. The best of the Lesser Antilles apprentices were sent to the mother countries for further training, therefore

the continuation of the same techniques were learned and carried forward on their return to the Antilles, making the distinction between port furniture and the locally made pieces sometimes a difficult one. Trade between the European countries and their colonies was restricted except by special treaties, so the free-ports were the only outlet the different and sometimes warring nations had to market their products.*

In France the ports of Bordeaux and La Rochelle received a tremendous amount of timber from the French Antilles, and the harbours of Le Havre were the shipping centre for the more exotic woods imported from the West Indies and the Americas. As a large and important port, Le Havre served much of the furniture trade in Paris and Europe, together with private purchases from France to the Antilles (see French Influence). Denmark used Flensberg** (see illustration and caption) as their port to produce furniture for their possessions in the Antilles. In the 1850s Flensberg became a German possession after the Schlswig-Holstein revolt between Denmark and Germany (1848–1850), but the Germans did not stop the trade of furniture to the Danish colonies. There was a definite German Baronial Revival influence which can be seen in a lot of the furniture in the homes of the Danish Antilles today. These pieces influenced the island artisans and the later nineteenth century items are made on a large scale reflecting this change.

Port furniture does not seem to have been a part of the development of furniture in the Dutch Antilles, as their colonies did not have any forests, but were mostly dry with few trees and shrubs. Pieces sent out from Holland that were intended for private houses became the models for some of the locally produced products. Their supply of hard woods were imported mainly from their colony of Surinam in South America. The American ports of Charleston, Boston and New York did import woods from the Antilles and furniture made there was sent back to the Antilles during the eighteenth and nineteenth century, especially to the free-ports, and also used as models by the local craftsmen.

Although furniture was imported into the Antilles during the nineteenth and twentieth century, the primary use of port factories diminished after the emancipation of slavery throughout the Lesser Antilles in the 1830s and 1840s, with the collapse of the 'Triangle Trade'. By this time the local trade had a monopoly on the market and pieces were made using the European form but the motifs and designs were used from design books, with the islands' flowers, plants and sea motifs, etc. used as popular examples.

* I am grateful to Susan Stuart for supplying information relating to the firm Gillows of Lancaster in this paragraph.

** Flensberg, 1833
Wharfside showing mahogany logs from the Danish West Indies ready to be made into furniture, for local and export use. A good deal of furniture made here was shipped back to the free-ports and the Danish West Indies.
(Print from the Schiffahrtsmusiem, Flensberg, Germany).

FINISHES, UPHOLSTERY AND CANING

Finishing is the least studied aspect of furniture but one of the most noticed. Old inventories tell us a lot about the different woods and when finishes are mentioned there is very little reference to them. They vary from region to region according to mixtures and applications. Over 200 different resins, fillers, oils, waxes and pigments that were used in the eighteenth, nineteenth and twentieth centuries have been recorded. Finishing was not a specialized trade in the furniture business until the restoration of antique furniture began in the twentieth century. Dyes, oils, stains, waxes, shellacs and paints were the main finishes used in the Antilles from 1740–1940 and some of these will be discussed here.

Oils, especially linseed and tung oil, were used to help preserve the woods and produced a rather matt finish when applied, rubbed and left to dry. This application was repeated several times until the piece of furniture had acquired a rich glow. Although this finish sank into the woods and did not sit on top as a protective coat, it had a certain appeal. There was no build up of a 'skin' so the wood was not protected from water, dust, scratches and other damaging elements.

Shellac, a form of varnish, was made from the resins of different insects then broken down and thinned out with alcohol and/or paraffin oil. It was then painted on, and usually two or three of these coats were applied, left to dry and lightly sanded between each application. (Before sandpaper was developed in 1860, fine sand under a damp cloth was used.) After three coats of this application the piece of furniture acquired a protective skin and rich high gloss.

Staining and dyeing before finishing was very popular especially with inlay work. The various woods used in marquetry and parquetry were dyed and stained to produce a close, natural effect for the design. If the marquetry design called for leaves, branches and flowers, then greens, browns, reds and yellows were used to create as lifelike a design as possible. Also, when pine, light-coloured and mixed woods were used to construct a piece, it would be stained a darker colour to hide the different woods and then usually finished with a hard skin. Among the different stains used in the Antilles, strong tea was used to obtain a mahogany colour. First the tea was stewed until very strong, then cooled and applied with a cloth to the piece of furniture. After it was allowed to dry, if the first coat was not deep enough, the application would be repeated until the required depth of finish was achieved. After that a finish coat was applied. Pieces of furniture used in the kitchens, bathrooms, pantries and in the sheds were sometimes stained without a finish coat such as pie safes, kitchen tables, plate racks, chairs and stools. Today there are modern stains which are much easier to use, allowing you to achieve the desired colour in one application.

French polishing was invented in France in 1810. It became very popular in Europe and spread to the rest of the world and is still used today. The principal ingredient in the process is 'lac' which is a resin-like substance excreted by a parasitic beetle (*laciffer iacoa*) living in certain trees in Asia. The resin is washed and melted to form flat, thin, two to three inch-wide discs. This lac is chemically

treated to achieve the different colours, such as brown, yellow, blonde and clear. There are several methods and mixtures for French polishing, the most popular being shellac mixed with linseed oil and muriatic acid on a piece of strong cotton or 'wadding', then applied to the wood in a curved and circular motion. This technique eliminates the brush strokes of the former application of shellac, the linseed oil making the cotton flow smoothly and the acid making sure that the lac is thinned out enough so that many applications are able to be applied over each other, until a beautiful skin is achieved.

An old piece of furniture that needs restoration usually has several layers of French polish making a thick skin, acquired over the lifetime of the piece. This old skin should not be stripped but cleaned. This skin has been acquired over many years and is expensive to replace. Light sanding and a few more applications of polish can restore the old finish. A less expensive manner used in the Antilles is to fill the wood grain. Plaster of Paris, pumice stone (an abrasive material made from volcanic ash) is used to help produce a fine finish between coats when binding the body of the finish and other natural clay-like materials are used with oil to fill the open grain and form the body before finishing. These can be stained or coloured and sometimes a binder of honey or linseed oil is used, then the application of two or three coats of the French Polish will produce a

Pitch Pine 'Caquetoire Gossip Chair', with a faux mahogany finish. Trinidad, *c.*1880.

Painted rocker and table. Barbados, *c.*1870. In original condition.

finish or shine that looks years older. French Polish produces a bright rich glowing finish that sometimes gives furniture a 'bejewelled' look.

Wax is also a finish and is very popular for a rich matt tone. Beeswax is the most popular wax, and with many applications over a long period of time can produce a very deep glowing shine. It is applied and left to dry for twenty-four hours and then buffed with a soft cloth. This process is repeated until the thickness of the finish and the glow is achieved. Beeswax is harvested from the hives and honeycombs of honeybees (*Apis Mellifera*), then processed and made into a paste.

Paint is a very popular finish in the West Indies. Painted furniture is often made from several pieces of different woods and scraps from the workshops mostly of semi-precious and base woods such as pine and oak. Suites of furniture used in the kitchens, storerooms, washhouses, bathrooms and pantries are often painted white or a pastel colour. Painted and polished over faux-finishes to simulate mahogany and other woods it is used in pine pieces such as, a wash stand that had to blend into an interior with other mahogany pieces. Painted finishes are easily wiped off when water is splashed on them. During the Arts and Crafts period, in the early twentieth century and onwards, entire bedroom and living-room suites were painted in pastel colours with matching upholstery. Many of these painted pieces have since been stripped, stained and polished to look like mahogany or other precious woods. Perhaps fashion trends will one day return these pieces to their original intended painted finish.

Rushing is one of the most ancient of crafts dating back at least 4,000 years to the ancient Egyptians. There are several boxes and a chest made from rush, papyrus and rush and reed in the Cairo Museum. China and Sumeria also record very early use of wicker. The raw materials were humble and easy to obtain. Baskets were functional and receptacles were made for every imaginable use. Bronze Age (8000 BC) remains have included rush work, as well as examples in Central and West Africa and Egypt dating from about 3000 BC. Rush work was used throughout Europe by the 1600s, and this art was developed in the Antilles, especially by the French settlers. Their old surviving chair seats are very fine. Rush and wicker is recorded in the Middle Ages in Europe, (*circa* 1400) and appeared in France and

Britain in the early 1700s. The English soon mastered the craft and improvements made during the Industrial Revolution brought the craft to an art form.

China is thought to have invented the caned chair which was brought westward to Europe by the China Trade and into England by the East India Company from the Malay peninsula. Cane is the hard outer bark of the rattan palm, a class of palms and related to the bamboo trees. The bark is stripped off and cut into a number of widths which has names such as binder, common, medium, fine, fine-fine, and super-fine. It was first introduced into England and Europe in the 1600s and then into the Antilles. The designs of the weaves are many with names like spiderweb 'A', using fine and medium canes. Then there is the 'daisy chain', 'daisy and buttons', 'double daisy' and various 'star and lace' patterns. This type of seating was very popular in the Antilles as it allowed the air to circulate around the body of the sitter and in the tropics was very welcome. Soon sofas, chaises-longues, stools, benches, armchairs, library chairs and anything you could sit or lie down upon was caned. This gave way to several shapes and designs being invented. The size of cane to be used is determined by the size of the holes on the seat, sides and back frames and their distance apart. Tools required are an awl, a sharp knife and a dozen wooden pegs. These pegs are to hold the ends until they are tied and to keep the strands taut during the weaving. The strands of cane are soaked in hot water so they are pliable during the weaving.

There are two methods of caning. The first is known as 'hand woven' which consists of weaving strands of cane through holes in the seat frame to form the desired pattern. The second is called a 'pressed seat' because the cane, woven in a desired pattern by a machine, is pressed into a groove in the seat frame and glued and fastened with a piece of reed called a 'spline'. Both of these techniques are old but the original is the method with the holes in the frame. Caning continues to be popular as a form of seating and the resurgence of interest in West Indian antique and reproduction furniture has made the craft available, once again.

Upholstery has played an important part in the history of European furniture from the sixteenth century to the present day. The earliest chairs were made with wooden seats and discomfort was relieved by a cushion. There were also leather seats and backs and squab cushions in the sixteenth and seventeenth centuries.

In the seventeenth, eighteenth and nineteenth centuries coverings became very fine using silk damask, needlepoint, petit-point and turkey work. Lavish use of trimmings was evident in seventeenth century upholstery especially in armchairs, stools and canopy beds. The canopy or tester protected the occupant from falling insects and the curtains provided privacy and warmth. These half-canopy and canopy beds developed into the four-poster bed, to become the most popular and prized piece of West Indian Furniture. The canopy and four-poster bed in the Caribbean was 'upholstered' with muslin and a muslin or lace fringe on the tester and repeated around the bottom of the bed. Mosquito netting hung all around the bed in draped, overlapping panels but during the day they were tied back to the bed posts. The mattress was usually made from horse-hair mixed with leaves and soft materials. The pillows were made from goose or swans' feathers and down. Braid was used to outline and emphasize the lines of the tester and crown.

The upholstered chair of the Antilles followed the styles and techniques of the mother country. Around 1750, a number of changes occurred; the basic components of webbing, curled hair linen and linen had not changed for years but now the designers started giving the seats different shapes. Not all upholstered seats were attached to the frame; some were 'drop-in', such as a serpentine upholstered frame that dropped into a groove. These changes happened with the introduction of horse-hair which became popular around that time and is still used today. About 1775, Indian cotton chintzes became popular, and soon challenged the Europeans', especially England's, textile industry. English mills soon started to print and became great producers of cotton products. These cotton textiles became popular in the Antilles because they were cool. Beds and windows, chairs and stools were draped in cotton, and the Creole belle wore the latest fashions in coloured and printed cottons. These cottons have continued to remain popular in the Antilles. French cottons finely printed in one or several colours on a pale background, are known as *toiles de Jouy* in France, after the factory of Jouy near Versailles. In addition to pastoral designs the factory produced designs with Chinese motifs and tropical flowers.

In 1830 the invention of the coil spring changed the history of upholstery. The shape of the seat was much thicker and more comfortable, leading to the overstuffed look during the remainder of the nineteenth century. The new seat was quickly adopted in the Lesser Antilles, as hot fashion over took cool comfort. Buttoning became a design detail on the backs, sides and seats of high sofas and armchairs. Some of these pieces of furniture had little or no wood showing, bringing the upholsterer to prominence. There was an increase in designs for upholstered furniture. Variations on the sofa and ottoman reached new heights of fancy. The 'tête-à-tête' sofa for seating a young unmarried couple with a chaperone in the middle was one such upholstered invention. This form has been recorded in the Antilles, both upholstered and caned. As with everything else, by 1860, the fabric designs had become confused. All the styles that went before were reused and recast and the last forty years of the nineteenth century saw a decline in the upholsterer and his art. By the twentieth century upholstery and textiles no longer dominated or mandated the decoration and design of a room. By this time the interior designer began to play an important role. Comfortable loose spring-cushioned chairs, like the ever-present and popular Morris chair (William Morris, 1834–1896), was adapted in the Antilles and has remained popular to this day.

TEA-TIME.
Saint Thomas, Saint Croix and Barbados furniture set out in a gallery with Anthurium Lilies. Afternoon tea was a popular pastime in the British Islands.

INTERIOR.
This interior shows a chaise-longue from Barbados, *circa* 1845, with ionic carved arm motif, carved and shaped back with leaf motif, and carved shaped tulip legs. It has a caned seat, back and side.
Collection: Matthew and Margaret Duensing.

71

Louis XV revival armoire. Purple Heart with Cyp panels and brass fiche/barrel hinges.

Louis XVI revival. Purple Heart armoire in neo-classical style. Trinidad, *c.*1850.

TROPICAL WOODS AND TIMBER
AVAILABLE TO THE MAKERS OF ISLAND FURNITURE

Bullet Wood

This genus, consists of over 150 species of evergreen trees and shrubs. It is noted for its latex which is the source of balata, a highly valuable article of commerce. The tree grows in tropical South America and the West Indies, being one of the largest tropical trees, growing to a height of over 150 feet. It has a rough scaly bark and a brown pulpy edible sweet fruit with one black seed. The leaves are dark green, oval in shape and two to four inches long.

This sapodilla fruit tree is rarely used in furniture making. It is extremely hard and heavy and is known as 'Bullet', 'Bully' and 'Balata' wood and is more commonly used for pilings and railway ties. It has an attractive grain and a colour of a rich reddish-brown darkening on exposure and it takes on an attractive finish. Because of the colour, it is sometimes called 'Beefwood' or 'Horse Flesh'. When it is used in furniture making it is easily worked, very heavy and takes on a silky shine. This tree is also called 'Mascotell' in the Virgin Islands.

HALF ROUND TABLE (One of a pair) 1825–1850.
Saint Thomas-Danish Influence. Ht.30" W.56" D.27½"
Bullet Wood with turned legs ending in brass cup toes and castors. Apron is cross-banded with Bullet Wood veneer on solid Bullet Wood. (Important)

CANTERBURY OR MUSIC STAND 1850–1875.
   Barbados-English Influence.
   Ht.29½" W.30" D.13½"
   Cedar, with pierced sides and separations, small drawer and scroll feet. (Important)

CHEST 1775–1799.
   Trinidad/Barbados-English Influence (Bermuda?).
   Ht.19¼" W.29½" D.20¾"
   Cedar with shaped feet and apron supporting a dovetailed box with moulded top. Brass handles.

Carapa

There are about a dozen species of Carapa, mostly in West Africa, South America and the West Indies. It is known as 'crabwood' in Guyana and 'Andrioba' in Brazil. It grows to a height of 120 feet, has a trunk diameter of up to three feet and enormous pinnate, compound leaves with numerous leathery opposite leaflets. The flowers are clustered and the globular fruit contains several seeds which are a source of oil used in the making of soap. When used on the skin, this oil also wards off mosquitoes. The timber is very popular in Guyana and is used for cabinet work. It gives readily, holds in place and is tough and strong for its weight. It is sometimes mistaken for mahogany but it lacks the richness and figuration of that wood. However, it is very suitable for furniture and is widely used in house construction, window sills, shingles, mortar, shipbuilding, mills and fencing.

Cedar

This genus consists of thirty or more species and is an important tropical South American tree. The wood is pinkish to red in colour, soft, easy to work, highly durable and has an agreeable fragrance which repels wood-boring worms and termites. The wood of the young trees that are of rapid growth is less fragrant, lighter in colour and softer than the old forest grown trees. Distribution ranges from Mexico, throughout the West Indies and Central and South America. The trees grow to a height of eighty to one hundred feet with a trunk diameter of up to six feet buttressed up to about ten feet. This trunk then grows straight up to the branches, some forty to sixty feet. The leaves are large and pinnate, the flowers small and the fruit capsules contain great quantities of winged seeds. Cedar has many uses in the tropics, being used in carpentry and construction work. The local uses include furniture, wardrobes, interiors and carcasses of large pieces of furniture. It is also used in interior fittings of rooms and innumerable small household articles. Trinidad exported Cedar to Europe and America for many years for use in furniture and cigar box manufacturing. When used on furniture the finish is smooth and takes a high shine with a pleasant appearance. As the tree has been heavily harvested it has become rare except in the more remote parts of the forest.

Courbaril (Hymenaea) (West Indian Locust)

This genus consists of about thirty species with the best known and most widely distributed being the West Indian Locust, one of the most valuable timber trees. It grows to a height of one hundred feet with a lofty spreading crown and an immense buttress trunk which grows up to a diameter of ten feet and has a long life. The leaves are large and thick with leaflets at the end of the stalk. 'Hymenaea' in the title is a reference to 'Hymen', the God of Marriage, as the white/purplish flowers are large and often used in bridal bouquets. The fruit is a thick-skinned pod with a few large seeds surrounded by a sweet pulp which is edible when ripe. The bark of the grown tree is sometimes an inch thick and is used by the Indians to make canoes. The wood is good quality and is used for carpentry, construction, boat-building, cabinet work and furniture. It is highly durable and is sometimes mistaken for mahogany. The colour of the wood ranges from orange to dark-brown with darker streaks that deepen upon exposure. The sapwood is dingy-white, yellowish or pink and the wood is tough and strong. It is not very easy to work, finishes smoothly but does not take a high polish. This wood has been over-harvested in the nineteenth century and it is extinct today in some of the West Indian Islands, making the furniture more desirable and expensive, particularly in the French-speaking islands where it is highly prized.

BEDROOM CORNER. FRENCH ANTILLES COURBARIL ARMOIRE of the Louis XVI period *circa* 1780. This piece is restrained and elegant with mahogany panels.

Courbaril rum table or high-legged console, Martinique *c.*1820.
Purple Heart scrolled-armed chair, St Croix *c.*1820.

Cyp

This genus, the most important of the family, consists of over 350 species of trees and shrubs. There are the light- and dark-coloured Cordias with the latter especially prized as cabinet woods. They are hard, heavy and variegated, with all shades of brown and markings of purple and black. They also have an oily appearance and feel with a pleasant scent. This tree grows to a height of fifty to eighty feet with a trunk diameter of twenty inches. It is also used in general construction and was formerly used in the making of vehicles and carts. The light Cordias are woods of general usefulness, ranging from light, soft and spongy to hard and heavy. The colours range from pale-yellow to light golden-brown and are variegated. This wood lacks the richness and figure of the darker groups but it is more abundant. It is used for general construction, cabinet work and furniture. It is easy to work, has a high lustre when polished and is sometimes used in Europe to replace oak. This tree has a wide range — from the West Indies and Mexico to Central and South America. This lighter variety grows up to seventy-five feet tall, with an eighteen to twenty-four inch trunk diameter and is remarkable for its thick clusters of large, long-lasting brown flowers and thin long leaves. It is very popular for making furniture in Trinidad and South America.

OBLONG CENTRE TABLE
1875–1889.
　Trinidad or Martinique-French Influence.
　Ht.29¾" W.27½" D.19"
　Cyp, with Walnut veneer decorative motifs. Turned and reeded legs and shaped cross-stretcher, with turned centre finial. Shaped apron with raised Walnut veneered motifs. Incised decoration on apron legs and stretcher. (Renaissance Revival, Important)

Douglas Fir (*Pseudosuga Menziesii*)

The Douglas Fir of the western United States, part of the extensive pine family, (also known as red fir, Oregon pine and abeto) extends into Mexico and is confined to high altitudes, ranging from 400-1,500 feet above sea level. The pine family is also abundant in Central America and the Dominican Republic, but most of the pines used in the Lesser Antilles are imported from North America. The pine family of woods is susceptible to termites and other wood-boring insects.

The heart is a light reddish-brown, with the edges a lighter colour. The wood is straight-grained, sometimes wavy and spiral, with a uniform medium texture. The wood works easily, as long as the tools are kept sharp. It is used for heavy construction work, interior joinery, marine piling, shipbuilding, furniture carcasses and entire pieces of furniture.

Ebony

This genus consists of a few American species of small trees and shrubs. It is native to the West Indies especially Jamaica, Cuba and Trinidad which supplies a limited quantity of small logs of the highly-prized wood known to the trade as Cocus Wood or West Indian Ebony. The tree is found in arid areas and grows to a height of twenty to fifty feet. Its trunk has a slim diameter of eighteen inches and it is covered with small thorns. The flowers are small and grow directly out of the trunk. It sheds its small leaves in the dry season and regrows them when it is rainy. As the tree is small and the heartwood is the only part used, this wood is rare. It is used to make flutes, clarinets and other musical instruments, inlay work, walking sticks and, rarely, small pieces of furniture. It is light-brown in colour with dark markings or streaks when newly cut but it becomes dark-brown to black with age. The wood contains a resin not unlike lignum-vitae, which makes it easy to work when it is newly cut. When it becomes black in colour it takes a high shine when polished.

BLANKET RACK 1875–1899.
Trinidad-English Influence.
Ht.62" W.47¾" D.12"
Douglas Fir with turned supports, finials and three rails on shaped feet.

Detail in ebony, crest carving, Trinidad, 1900.

'SUTHERLAND' GATELEG
TABLE 1875–1900.
Trinidad/Barbados-English
(Sheraton revival).
Ht.22" W.22¼" D.51/2" (open
25⅝")
Mahogany, mahogany veneer,
Cedar, Satinwood, Ebony and
Green Heart, with six turned
legs. Mahogany veneer on cedar
top with inlaid cross-banding of
Ebony and Satinwood on top
edge. Centre motif inlaid with
Ebony, Satinwood and Green
heart. Legs are made of Cedar.

The Sutherland table was
invented by the Duchess of
Sutherland, England in the
1780s, to reside next to her
armchair where, as an invalid,
she sat for long periods. This
can be called the forerunner of
the T.V. table.

Lignum-vitae tree.

Green Heart
This species is not found in the West Indies and is imported mostly from Guyana
and tropical South America. It is a large evergreen tree ranging from seventy to 120
feet high, three to four feet in diameter and sometimes even larger. The trunk rises
straight up until it reaches between fifty to seventy feet where it then branches out.
The leaf stalks are short, the leaf thick and leathery, and the flower is small,
yellowish-white and with a fragrance suggesting the scent of jasmine. The wood is
hard, heavy and dense and is mostly used for boardwalks, piers and pilings. Other
uses have been automobile spokes, carriage shafts and fishing rods. It is immune to
termites and water rot. The colour ranges from light- to dark-olive to nearly black.
The sapwood is pale-yellow and is extremely durable. Furniture made from this
variety is very expensive and a rare find in the West Indies. This wood is also known
as Brown, Black, White, Yellow and Green wood.

Lignum Vitae (*Guaiacum officinale*)
Lignum-vitae or 'guaiacum' is well-represented in the West Indies. The evergreen
tree is usually less that thirty feet high and has a trunk only twelve inches in diameter
although there are some exceptions of larger trees. The leaves are small and it bears
a cluster of bluish-purple flowers. The wood is very hard and has to be worked
before it has a chance to dry. It has great strength and tenacity which makes it usable
for underwater bearings, chisel blocks, caster wheels and clock cogs. It is also used
for marquetry and parquetry on furniture. It has been used in Europe since the
early sixteenth century and considered expensive and valuable. It has the nickname
of 'poxwood', because the medical profession in Europe believed it had remedial
powers, using it to treat syphilis, and other serious diseases. The name 'Lignum-
Vitae' ('wood of life') had such a firm reputation for its curing powers, that it was
written about extensively. After three hundred years of using this wood as a medical
treatment it was finally questioned and is now medicinally obsolete.

Mahogany (*Swietenia mahogoni*).
(The mahogany family is a vast one. The information below is concerned with only one genus, as it is indigenous to the West Indies.)

The Mahogany family consists of about forty genera and over six hundred species of trees, shrubs and woody herbs, distributed throughout both tropical hemispheres. There are six important genera in tropical America and the West Indies. Swietenia, with five known species is the only source of true mahogany, and is the premier cabinet wood of the world. It was used by Cortez to build ships for further voyages of discovery and conquest, from Santo Domingo. Sir Walter Raleigh repaired his ship in Trinidad in 1595, and is credited with introducing mahogany to England, the story being that he presented a mahogany table to Queen Elizabeth I.

All the mahogany in the West Indies is the product of a single species *Swietenia mahogoni*. Although there are mahogany trees throughout the Lesser Antilles, they are not indigenous as they were brought here from British Jamaica, French and Dutch Guyana and Spanish America. This mahogany of the West Indies may be considered the standard for the group and is the kind

INTERIOR, showing a mahogany armoire of Louis XVI influence with four flush panels inlaid with Zebra Wood outlining the panels on the doors. Curaçao *circa* 1850. Collection: Corrine Lockhart.

that was used exclusively in furniture. This is known as 'Antiques in Mahogany.'

The mahogany is a stately and beautiful tree and can attain large dimensions, often over one hundred feet in height. It has a straight trunk, four to six feet in diameter, above a heavy buttress and branches out at forty to sixty feet. The pinnate leaves are in pairs, smooth and shiny and the flowers are small, white and purple. The fruit is a large pod measuring two by six inches with numerous seeds. Mahogany is the most valuable timber tree in Tropical America and is the standard by which other cabinet woods are compared. It is known for its richness in colour, enhanced by age, its deep lustre and great beauty of grain and figuring. It is durable, finishes smoothly, and can be used in solid form or as a veneer. It is a luxury timber for cabinets, furniture and all purposes in carpentry and joinery.

'Mahogany Trees' and 'Mahogany Alley'.

Machineel (*Hippomane Mancinella*)

The Manchineel is a single genus species, ranging from the West Indies through Central and South America. It grows to a height of sixty-five feet with a trunk of three feet in diameter. It has simple, large leaves and a fruit that resembles an apple. The bark has a thick milky juice that is poisonous and causes eruptions upon contact with the skin. It is used for wainscoting and cabinets. The wood is much coveted for its durability. The colouring is a delicate and lustrous yellowish-brown, suggesting walnut, and it takes a high polish. To be able to fell the tree, a fire has to be made around it so the bark with the poisonous sap is burned off.

Pine

Pines are the most important group of timber trees in North America, and are confined to temperate regions. Pine is a large family including white, foxtail, nut and pitch pines. It is found on several West Indian Islands but it is most abundant in the Dominican Republic. The tree grows to a height of forty to sixty feet with a trunk diameter of twenty-five inches. They are usually found growing in dense pure stands in the forests. Up to ninety percent of the pine used in the Lesser Antilles is imported from North America. Many of the buildings in the Lesser Antilles are built mostly from this wood and white pine due to the trade with the east coast of America. The heart of this particular pitch pine repels termites and other wood-boring insects because of the hardness it achieves with age but the rest stays soft and is attacked.

This wood is coloured from orange to reddish-brown. It is easily worked, but the resin can blunt tools quickly. The finishing treatments and polishes are satisfactory. It is used for heavy construction such as spars, masts, flooring, crates, joinery, furniture and furniture carcasses. Resin and turpentine are produced from this species.

Purple Heart

This genus consists of a dozen or more species ranging from Mexico to Brazil and the larger West Indian Islands, especially Trinidad. The tree can grow to a height of 125 feet with a trunk diameter of up to four feet and branches extending fifty feet. It has leathery leaves with twin leaflets, as in 'Hymenaea', with small, white flowers and wood famous for its purple colour upon exposure to air. It can become very dark with age and its sapwood is white with purple streaks. It has great strength and toughness and is used to make spokes for cartwheels, mortar beds and other purposes where shock resistance is needed. It is used for furniture inlay work and turnery and is popular in Europe for cabinetmaking. There is a grand staircase in Stollmeyer's Castle in Trinidad made exclusively of this wood from Guyana. Whole pieces of furniture made of this wood are rare and highly-prized. The grain is mostly straight, sometimes wavy or roey*. The wood is fine-textured, strong and durable, it takes a high polish and produces a smooth finish. This wood is also popularly called 'Amarante' or 'Violetwood' in Europe.
(* The spotty appearance of fish eggs.)

ARMCHAIR 1800–1825.
  St Croix-Danish Influence.
  Ht.23" W.20" D.18"
  Purple Heart Wood, with turned and reeded legs, scrolled arms, carved splat, and drop-in upholstered seat. (Important and rare)

Collection of Pitch Pine furniture from Barbados – Chair 1900, Plant Stand 1940, Display Unit, 1890.

ROCKING CHAIR 1875–1899.
St Thomas-French Influence.
Ht.38" W.23¼" D.33"
Mahogany, Pine, Saman, Thibet,
Red Oak, White Oak and
Crappo.
Louis XVI revival featuring
carved leaf and scrolled motif,
oval inserted back, supported by
scrolled stretcher, with shaped
and scrolled arms, ending in
turned supports with finials.
Round caned seat, and shaped
apron, turned front legs and
stretchers. Note: this piece was
stained with strong tea to get an
even-looking Mahogany finish,
then French polished.
(Important)

Red Oak

The heart is similar to other oaks, and
has a beige to pink colour, with a red
tint. It is straight-grained and coarse,
and has smaller rays than white oak. The
heart wood is soft, liable to insect attack
and resistant to preservative treatment.
It is used for flooring, interior joinery
and furniture but is unsuitable for
exterior work.

Roble Wood

This genus consists of about twenty-five species of shrubs and trees growing in
tropical America and Trinidad. The leaves are whorled, with leaflets and are large.
The flowers are yellow and the fruit or pods are flat and do not open. It is a small,
semi-deciduous tree, that grows to one hundred feet in height.

This wood is part of the West Indian oak family An extremely hard and heavy
wood, it is not often used in the making of furniture, therefore the pieces found are
rare and the pieces known were custom-made on estates by their craftsmen. This
wood was mainly used for floorings and staircases. The early French settlers in Haiti
crafted furniture from this wood and the pieces are considered works of art. Also
known as 'Catalpa', this reddish-brown wood with purplish streaks takes on a lovely
polish with a rich hue. It is a small semi-deciduous tree, that grows to one hundred
feet in height and is found throughout the Antilles.

ARMOIRE 1875–1900.
Trinidad/Martinique-French Louis XVI revival.
Ht.104" W.39¼" D.24"
Made from Roble Wood (tabebuia) and Cedar. It has a single door with a bevelled-
shaped mirror and brass escutcheon. A pair of carved reeded and turned columns,
topped by urn finials are free-standing on square moulded and carved plinths. The
bottom encloses a drawer which stands on four turned legs. The entire piece is
surmounted by a bonnet top, carved and reeded with applied mouldings of Cedar.
On top of this is a carved leaf and flower motif around a beaded shield.

STANDING SCREEN (Set of three) 1900–1925. Art Nouveau.

Trinidad-English and Indian Influence.
Ht.86¾" W.45" D.15" (large screen); Ht.86¾" W.24" D.15" (small pair)
Rosewood with moulded and panelled bottom and centre with louvered top, crowned with a filigree carved and pierced tiara. This filigree is reminiscent of the jewellery brought to Trinidad by the East Indians in the 1840s and onwards. These screens were part of the original furnishings of Stollmeyer's Castle in Port of Spain, Trinidad.

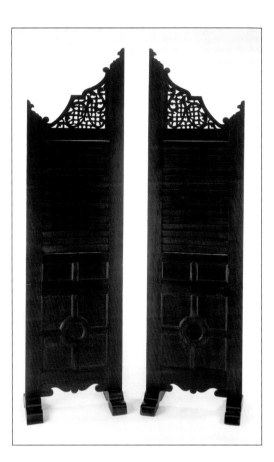

Rosewood

Rosewood is one of the most famous woods of the tropics especially of French Guyana and has been used in France for a long time in the production of furniture. In 1875, France distilled its sweet-smelling oils for the use in perfume-making. The tree grows scatteredly in mixed hardwood forests and is tall and slender. The trunk is straight and cylindrical and covered in a flaky bark. The inner bark is very fragrant, light-brown and soft. The top of the tree is very small with thick upright branches, leaves that are about seven inches long and three inches wide, with the upper part green and the underneath brown and velvety. The colour of the wood is a lustrous yellow turning to a rich brownish-red on the surface. The odour of the freshly worked wood is pronounced, smelling and tasting somewhat like nutmeg. It crafts beautifully into furniture and when finished the wood takes on a special golden hue. Furniture made in the West Indies from Rosewood is highly prized, especially in the French Islands.

STAND 1875–1900.
Flensberg, Denmark German Influence.
Ht.36½" D.12¾"
Oak with spiral-turned support, round top, round base on four carved 'goat hoof' toes.
Collection: Gwendolyn Kean.

CONSOLE TABLE 1800–1825.
Trinidad-Louis XV Influence.
Ht.39¼" W.62¼" D.18¾"
Saman with serpentine-shaped
top of white marble, shaped
apron, with raised carved flower
garland design across front, on
four cabriole legs with carved
flowers and scrolls on knees and
ending with scrolled toes.
(Important)

Saman (*Enterolobium* 'Saman Prain')

This genus has five different species. The wood is very close in appearance to the West Indian Walnut. The Saman or Rain Tree is indigenous to South America and is planted to shade cocoa and coffee trees. It is often planted in open spaces and pastures to provide shade and its fallen fruit provides forage for cattle. It grows an enormous, umbrella-shaped canopy spread of over one hundred feet in diameter. The trunk has a diameter of up to eight feet and grows to a height of seventy to one hundred feet. The wood is light and soft, and varies from easy to cut to being hard, heavy and fibrous in the older trees. The colour ranges from golden-brown to deep-chocolate, in large stripes. The wood is used for canoes, water troughs, carpentry and cabinet work.

The crown has large, finely pinnate leaves. The flowers are small, in white and yellow clusters and the fruits are black leathery pods with three to five seeds and shaped like a human ear. The fruit and bark are used for medicinal purposes in the treatment of colds and bronchitis.

The distinctive shape of a Saman Tree with its enormous, umbrella-shaped canopy.

Sand Box

This tree, the most important of the two species of this genus, grows throughout tropical America and the West Indies and is favoured as a decorative and a shade tree. It has several names, the most popular in the Lesser Antilles is the Sand Box Tree. It grows to one hundred feet high, with a large limbed spreading crown and a trunk up to nine feet in diameter. The bark is smooth except for the conical prickles of the lower portion of the trunk giving the tree the local name of 'monkey puzzle tree' or 'monkey no climb'. The leaves have prominent ribs and are dull on both surfaces. The dark red flowers bloom in large clusters and the fruit is a woody capsule about three inches across and shaped like a small pumpkin. When ripe, they burst sending their seeds in all directions. The old West Indian practice of hollowing out the immature fruit and filling it with blotting sand gave the tree the name 'Sand Box Tree'. The shape of the fruit was copied as a feature for furniture decoration, usually instead of bun feet and simple turnings. This feature was largely used on Barbados furniture of the late Regency period and onwards. In Trinidad the tree is very common, with sometimes up to forty trees to an acre. The wood is used widely for boxes, crates, and all sorts of inexpensive cabinetry work. The sap of the bark is irritating to the eyes making the tree an unpopular working wood. When used it is a substitute for soft woods, has a high silky lustre, takes stains readily and has enough figure for cabinet work.

PRINT.

Depiction of the Sand Box Tree found in Barbados. This motif is found on Barbados furniture and the tree grows throughout the Lesser Antilles. English, *circa* 1780.

CANDLE OR PLANT STAND

1850–1875.
Barbados-Local and English Influence.
Ht.25¼" D.9½"
Mahogany with pedestal of ring turns and a carving of a sand box motif.
Circular foot and top.

PARTNERS' KNEEHOLE DESK
1775–1800.
   Barbados-English/Sheraton
   Influence.
   Ht.31¼" W.42" D.27¼"
Mahogany, Mahogany Veneer, Cedar,
Satinwood. This desk is veneered with
Mahogany over Cedar. The top, sides,
legs and drawers are inlaid with Satinwood in a string design. Both front
and back have the same design of four
drawers and a cupboard, the drawers
have wooden handles. The kneehole
has a shaped design on four tapered
legs with brass castors. (Important)

CUPPING/RUM TABLE 1850–1875.
St Thomas/St Croix-Danish
Influence.
Ht.45½" W.34½" D.22"
This cupping/bar table is made from
Thibet wood with a Pine sub-structure.
The front drawer with wooden handles
has a scalloped-designed bottom which
carries throughout the sides. The legs
have turned ball, ring, and urn
designs. The top has a spindled gallery
and shaped cut-out and mirrored back.
These tables sometimes came in pairs
or fours and were placed in the public
rooms.

Satinwood
The satinwood family has about 110 genera and consists of over 1,000 species of
trees and shrubs world-wide. The West Indian satinwood family includes 200
species of trees and shrubs and is most abundant in tropical America and the West
Indies. These trees are small to medium size, growing to about fifty feet in height
with trunks up to eighteen inches in diameter. Out of these, at least two species
contribute to the supply of commercial West Indian satinwood. Its range includes
Santo Domingo, Puerto Rico, Bermuda and Trinidad in the West Indies. The
wood is hard, heavy, fine textured with a beautiful wavy grain and of a creamy or
golden yellow colour, giving off a pronounced scent of coconut when freshly
worked. It is used for fine furniture, cabinetwork, inlay, marquetry, parquetry,
turnery and brush backs. Most of the antique satinwood furniture is made almost
exclusively from this wood because of its availability. Another kind of West Indian
satinwood is known as 'Concha Satinwood'. It is coarser in texture, less heavy and
firm, is dull-brown without much scent but it is beautifully figured and gives an
attractive effect and shine when made into furniture. Another group of satinwood
known as 'Z. Martinicenses' is one of the largest trees. It grows up to seventy feet
in height and has a reddish-yellow streaked wood, used for furniture, cabinet work
and construction and is called 'prickly ash' in the British Islands. Furniture made
of solid satinwood is highly-prized, especially the pieces made in the West Indies.

Tamarind
This tree grows throughout the Antilles, to a considerable size — sometimes to
120 feet in height. Its double-pinnate leaves are bright green, large, often sixteen
inches long, with numerous pinnate and fine linnear leaflets. The flowers are
white and the fruit is a brown pod with black seeds and a bitter taste. The wood
has the general appearance of mahogany (*Swietenia*), and some is beautifully
figured. It is used for furniture, flooring, ceilings, posts and general construction.

Thibet

Also known as Indian Walnut, from a large family, Thibet Wood is grown in all tropical countries. The tree grows to a height of one hundred feet, and a diameter of thirty to forty feet, with large spreading branches forming an umbrella, making it a good shade tree. The flowers are small and white, with pods shaped like the human ear. The large trunks are used for canoes, water troughs and in carpentry and cabinet work. The pods are good fodder for cattle and the seeds are cooked for human food. The fruit is used as a soap substitute and the trunk gum used as a remedy for bronchitis. The colour is walnut-brown, with various shadings and sometimes with a red hue. It is easy to work, and takes a high polish.

Walnut

The walnut family supplies some of the most valuable and widely used timber in the world. Although widespread throughout Europe and Asia, we are concerned here with the variety that grows in tropical America and the West Indies. The wood portrays wide variations in colour, from black to butternut to golden walnut. It grows in the mountainous areas of the tropics and the most popular for cabinetwork is the butternut variety. The butternut tree grows to a height of eighty feet with a twenty-four inch diameter of the trunk. The wood is lighter in weight than the black varieties and the bark and sawdust are used widely for dyes, giving a coffee-brown colour. The butternut wood is mostly seen as panels for cabinets or wardrobes used in contrast to dark wood frames. It is easy to work, holds its shape, takes a high finish with a satiny lustre and is strong and durable.

Zebra Wood

Zebra Wood is a rare tree that grows in South America and Trinidad. It grows to a height of fifty feet with a trunk diameter of twenty-four inches and a heavy buttressed base. The bark is rough, leaves are double-pinnate and its small yellow flowers grow in bunches. The fruit is a pod of about five inches long and is curved. The wood is light-brown with an irregular black and purple striped grain. This pattern makes a bold statement of design with the lighter lines throughout. The wood is strong and tough, difficult to work, but finishes smoothly and takes a high polish. It is a valuable wood in Europe and is mostly used for inlay work. Any discovery of a solid piece of furniture made from this wood is a rare and precious event.

ARMOIRE 1800-1825.
Trinidad/Martinique-Louis XV Influence.
Ht.70" W.47½" D.20½"
This small armoire is made of Mahogany, Courbaril and West Indian Walnut. The shaped door frames are made from Courbaril enclosing panels of Walnut. It has a moulded, shaped and rounded-corner cornice and two mahogany panels on each side. It stands on shaped cabriole legs and ends in scrolled toes with a shape apron on the bottom, front and sides. It has brass fiche/barrel hinges and escutcheons. (Important)

CARD OR GAME TABLE 1800–1825.
  Barbados-English Influence.
  Ht.28" W. 36" D 18"
  Mahogany, Cedar and Zebra Wood. Turned cedar column and broken sabre legs inlaid with Zebra Wood, ending in brass toes. Zebra Wood inlay also decorates the apron, edges and top which is veneered in Mahogany. (Important)

INTERIOR.
  Large Mahogany and Cedar breakfront cabinet with four shaped and glazed doors, with carved corbels below the moulded top and drawers. The drawers are hidden in the bottom half of the cabinet with four shaped panelled doors on a solid platform. Barbados *circa* 1875.

THE COLLECTION

INTERIOR.
  Corner of sitting-room showing Mahogany chaise-longue with caning and loose cushions. *circa* 1875.
  Collection: Adrian Camps-Campins

DINING CHAIRS (One of a pair) 1825–1850.
   Barbados-English Influence.
   Ht.35" W.17" D.16"
   Mahogany, with turned and octagonal-shaped legs, 'ginger bread'-style splat and caned seat.

ROCKING CHAIR 1850–1875.
   Barbados or Trinidad-English Influence.
   Ht.40" W.22" D.33"
   Mahogany, with shaped back, turnback scrolled arms, turned front legs and stretcher. Caned seat and back.

ARMCHAIR (One of a pair) 1850–1875.
   Trinidad or Martinique-French Influence.
   Ht.37" W.17" D.18"
   Mahogany, Louis XVI Revival, caned back and seat, turned and reeded legs, shaped seat. Possibly library chairs.
   (Important)

DINING CHAIRS (One of a pair) 1825–1850.
  Trinidad or Martinique-English Influence.
  Ht.33" W.16" D.17"
  Mahogany, with turned legs, caned seat, simple
  splat on a sweeping back.

ROCKING CHAIRS (One of a pair) 1900–1925.
  Barbados-English Influence.
  Ht.36" W.20" D.25"
  Mahogany, with turnback arms, oval-shaped back (influenced by
  Thornet's Bentwood), cabriole legs, paw feet. Caned seat and
  back. This pair of rockers have a rare maker's label on the
  underside of the back rail.
  'Manufactured by C. F.Harrison & Co. Ltd. Barbados W.I.'

ARMCHAIR (One of a pair) 1800–1825.
  Trinidad or Barbados-English Influence.
  Ht.33" W.22" D.17"
  Mahogany, sabre legs, scrolled arms and carved back, splat and rail.
  Note the bell-flower motif on the top rail. (Important) Provenance:
  Lord Harris, Governor of Trinidad in the 1830s and 1840s

DETAIL of back of Dining chair with bow splat and gadrooned back rail

DINING CHAIRS (Set of six) 1825–1850.
  Barbados-English Influence.
  Ht.34" W.19" D.16"
  Mahogany, turned and reeded legs, caned seat, carved bow-tie motif splat, and gadrooned back rail. (Important)

ROCKING CHAIR 1850–1875.
  St Croix-Danish Influence.
  Ht.38" W.22" D.35"
  Mahogany, with caned seat and back, scrolled arms, shaped feet and turned stretcher. This design originated in the 1830s and has been made ever since.

ROCKING CHAIR (One of a pair) 1850–1875.
  St Croix-Danish Influence.
  Ht.39" W.22" D.34"
  Mahogany, with caned seat and back, scrolled arms and shaped stretcher

DINING CHAIRS (Set of four) 1775–1800.
  Barbados-English Influence.
  Ht.38" W.20" D.17"
  Mahogany, Hepplewhite influence, shield-back, with carved and pierced splat. Tapered legs with shoes, and drop-in upholstered seats. (Important)

DINING CHAIRS (Set of four)
1800–1825.
    Barbados or Trinidad-English
    Influence.
    Ht.32" W.18" D.16"
    Mahogany, with sabre legs,
    carved splat, turned top rail and
    drop-in upholstered seat.

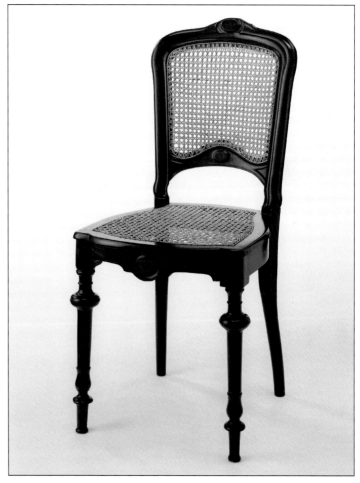

CHILD'S CHAIR 1900–1925.
    Trinidad or Barbados-English Influence.
    Ht.33" W.16" D.16"
    Mahogany, Satinwood and Cedar. Sheraton revival with
inlaid top rail and string inlay on back posts and splat, with
turned legs and upholstered seat.

DINING CHAIR (One of a pair) 1850–1875.
    St Croix-French Influence.
    Ht.33" W.18" D.18"
    Mahogany, with turned legs, shaped and carved apron,
back and seat, caning on back and seat.

INTERIOR.

Mahogany, French-style Louis XV revival dresser, with serpentine-shaped front, panelled sides and marble top. Carved and reeded corner posts, with carved front of drawers with wooden knobs. Oval mirror on carved naturalistic supports, compartment in base, also in Mahogany. The pieces are from either Martinique or Trinidad, *circa* 1875.

VERANDA SETTING
  A Trinidad, Louis XIV influence double-caned armchair, a Grenadian plant stand and a Cruzan side table in an early evening setting for a glass of sherry.

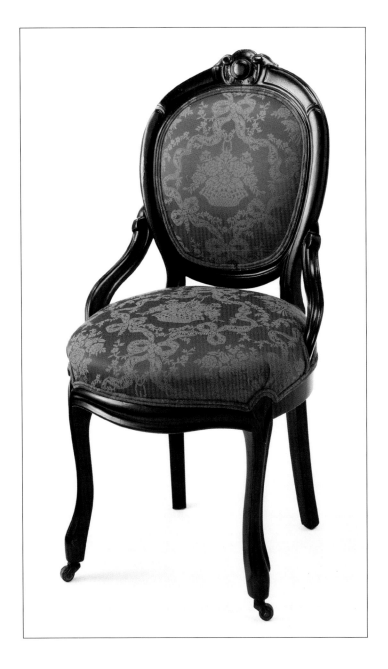

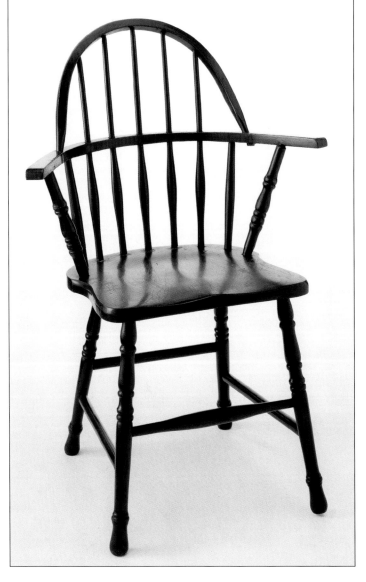

BOUDOIR CHAIR 1875–1899.
   Barbados or Trinidad-French Influence.
   Ht.37" W.19" D.19"
   Mahogany, with upholstered seat and back, carved and shaped frame throughout.

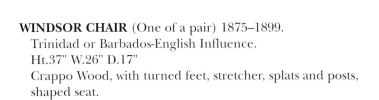

WINDSOR CHAIR (One of a pair) 1875–1899.
   Trinidad or Barbados-English Influence.
   Ht.37" W.26" D.17"
   Crappo Wood, with turned feet, stretcher, splats and posts, shaped seat.

TEA TABLE 1750–1775.
   Barbados-English Influence.
   Ht.26½" D.24¼"
   Mahogany, with turned and carved pedestal, with snakehead tripod feet.
   Saucer tip-top with original hardware. (Important)

BERGERE CHAIR (above)
1800–1825.
   Barbados-French/English
   Influence.
   Ht.36" W.24" D.24"
   Mahogany, with turned
   and reeded front posts and
   legs, shaped and fluted
   arms into square and
   fluted back. Caned seat,
   inner arms and back. Also
   with brass toes and castors.

DETAIL of inlay over caning
channel on arm rest and
support of Bergere chair

BERGERE CHAIR (One of a pair, top, left) 1875–1900.
   Barbados-French/English Influence.
   Ht.37" W.24" D.20"
   Mahogany, with turned front posts, and tapered legs, curved
   arms and square back and seat. Caned seat, inside arms and
   back. A style that was started in the early 1800s and emulated
   into the 1900s.

ARMCHAIR 1800–1825.
   St Croix-Danish Influence.
   Ht.23" W.20" D.18"
   Purple Heart Wood, with turned and reeded legs, scrolled arms,
   carved splat, and drop-in upholstered seat. (Important and rare)

CHILD'S HIGH CHAIR 1825–1850.
Barbados or Trinidad-English Influence.
Ht.34" W.14" D.18"
Mahogany, with turned legs, stretcher and arm supports, shaped and carved arms and back splat and caned seat.

MASTER ARMCHAIR 1875–1899
Trinidad-French Influence, Louis XIV
Ht.48" W.23½" D.19"
Mahogany and Cedar. Turned legs, shaped arms, carved and shaped back with turned finials on back posts and carved cresting on back. Caned seat and double-caned back (French style).

NIGHT CHAIR
1825–1850.
Barbados-English
Influence.
Ht.34½" W.22" D.17"
Mahogany, with turned
legs, turned and
shaped arms and
carved splat.
Clay and glazed potty.

ARMCHAIR (Pair) 1800–1825.
Barbados-English Sheraton Influence.
Ht.32" W.21¾" D.17¼"
Mahogany, with turned legs and arm posts, shaped arms,
simple splat and caned seat.

DINING CHAIR 1850–1875.
Trinidad or Barbados-English Influence.
Ht.34" W.22" D.17"
Mahogany, with turned legs, shaped back, carved splat and
caned seat.

LIBRARY CHAIR 1825–1850.
  Barbados-English Influence.
  Mahogany, with turned and reeded legs, acanthus carved arm supports and scrolled arm rests. Caned back, seat and sides.

CANDLESTAND 1875–1899.
  St Thomas-Danish Influence.
  Ht.29" W.21" D.14½"
  Mahogany, with turned column and fretted tripod, rectangular top with shaped apron.

OUTDOOR SETTING.
Featuring a nineteenth century plant stand from Barbados supporting a plume of tropical orchids.

SOFA 1800–1825.
Barbados-English Regency Influence.
Ht.34½" W.92" D.23"
Made from Mahogany with Pine sub-structure, with upholstered back, arms, seat and bolsters. The scrolled arms have reeded motifs which continue throughout the surfaces of the entire piece. The back is also carved and reeded. It stands on four scrolled and reeded legs, ending in brass claw toes and castors. (This sofa is rare and important and is a high watermark in West Indian antique furniture.)

CHEVAL MIRROR 1850–1875.
Trinidad/Martinique-Louis XVI Revival.
Ht.71¼" W.30½" D.22¼"
Mahogany and Cedar with shaped mirror frame, carved bow and crest ornament, suspended on square-panelled poles, with brass swings and turned finials. The stand and platform have turned and fluted legs, ending in brass castors. (Important)

FOUR-POSTER BED 1825–1850.
Martinique/Barbados/Grenada-English/French Influence.
Ht.86" W.91" D.64"
Solid Mahogany with leaf carving, turned, twist turns, reeded urns on the posts, and ending with turned and reeded legs. The back is profusely carved with palm leaf motifs and has shaped stretchers.

NIGHT STAND 1825–1850.
  Barbados-English Influence.
  Ht.29½" W.24" D.18"
  Mahogany, Satinwood, and Pine, with turned legs and insert
  columns, crossbanding inlaid work around drawers and false
  front, wooden knobs.

TEA TABLE
1750–1775.
  Barbados-English
  Influence.
  Ht.30" D.24"
  Mahogany, tip-top
  with turned pedestal,
  and carved tripod
  and club feet.
  Collection: Russell
  Prendergast.
  (Important)

DETAIL shows flowers,
leaf and fern tendril.

TEA TABLE *c.*1775–1779.
Barbados-English Influence.
Ht.28" D.27½"
Mahogany 'Chippendale' tea table with tip-top. Turned tripod
pedestal with flower and fern motif on knees ending with claw and
ball feet.

TEA TABLE 1775–1779.
Barbados-English Influence.
Ht.27½" D.27"
Mahogany, with turned and carved tripod ending in snakes head
feet, carved fern tendrils and sea grape leaves on knees. Carved pie-
crust top sits on a box known as a birdcage. (Important)

A MORRIS ARMCHAIR (From a suite of three Morris armchairs and Settee)
1930 – Art Deco.
Barbados-English Influence.
Ht.28" W.25¾" D.34"
Mahogany, with low slung slat formation on seat and back, oval-shaped and carved arms with pierced splat decoration. Built for upholstered cushions

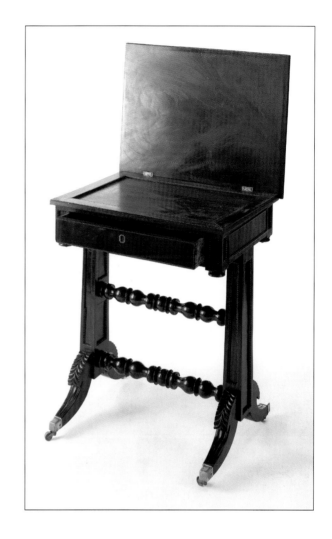

WRITING DESK 1825–1850.
  Barbados-English Influence.
  Ht.29½" W.24" D.17"
  Mahogany, Mahogany Veneer, and Cedar. Turned stretchers into
  panelled uprights, supported by two broken sabre legs carved with a
  palm design, and finishing with brass toes. This piece has bead
  moulding throughout the panelling on the front, the sides and
  uprights. The top opens to reveal a writing area.

WINE CELLARET 1825–1850.
  Barbados-English Influence.
  Ht.30½" W.27" D.18"
  Mahogany, with Cedar interior, and panelled front and sides, turned
  legs, and a brass bounded top with carrying handles on the sides.
  Reminiscent of military campaign chests.

CARD OR GAME TABLE
1800–1825.
Barbados-English Influence.
Ht.30" W.37" D.18"
Mahogany and Satinwood,
with reeded and turned
column, spurred reeded sabre
legs, ending in brass toes.
Reeded apron and string
inlaid design on top.
(Important)

CARD OR GAME TABLE
1800–1825.
    Barbados-English Influence.
Ht.28" W. 36" D 18"
Mahogany, Cedar and Zebra
Wood. Turned cedar column
and broken sabre legs inlaid
with Zebra Wood, ending in
brass toes. Zebra Wood inlay
also decorates the apron, edges
and top which is veneered in
Mahogany. (Important)

DINING CHAIRS (set of ten) 1825–1845.
Barbados-English Influence.
Ht.34" W.19" D.16"
Mahogany, with reeded and turned legs, caned seat,
reeded and turned back rail and carved panelled top rail.

MUSIC STAND
1825–1850.
Trinidad or Barbados-
French Influence.
Ht.31" W. 15"
Mahogany, with fluted
carved and turned
tripod pedestal and
carved cabriole legs
ending in reverse scroll
feet (missing top for
music sheet).

CANDLESTAND
1875–1895.
St Thomas-Danish
Influence.
Ht.29¾" W.31" D.13½"
Mahogany, column-
turned with urn, ball
and ring designs and
carved and shaped
tripod ending in reverse
scroll feet. Shaped top
and apron.

CANTERBURY OR MUSIC STAND
1850–1875.
  Barbados-English
  Influence.
  Ht.29½" W.30" D.13½"
  Cedar, with pierced sides
  and separations, small
  drawer and scroll feet.
  (Important)

PEDESTAL TABLE
1800–1825.
  England-Port Furniture
  (note influence on
  No 34)
  Ht.26½" W.23"
  Mahogany, with reeded
  and turned pedestal and
  reeded sabre leg tripod,
  ending in brass toes.
  Circular top with moulded
  edge. Note: stamped twice,
  'Gillows' and 'Lancaster', a
  famous export firm to the
  West Indies.

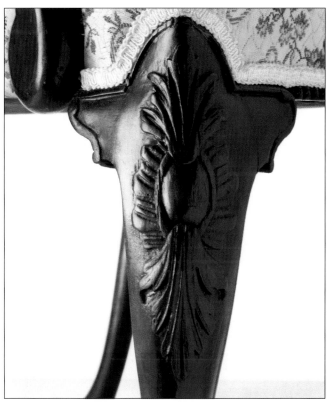

ARMCHAIR 1750–1775.
  Barbados-English Influence.
  Ht.37" W.22½" D20"
Mahogany, with carved cabriole legs, knee decoration
and ending in claw and ball feet. The back is carved
with a pierced and scrolled splat, and curved arms.
This chair started life as a single, maybe from a long
set, and acquired its arms about 100 years later. An
evolutionary piece.

ARMCHAIR 1730–1750.
Barbados-English 'Queen Anne' Influence.
Ht.37" W.23" D.19"
Mahogany, shaped back and splat with curved arms and upholstered drop-in seat. The cabriole legs have shell and scroll carved decorations on the knees, ending in shallow pad feet. (Important)

FOLDING DECK CHAIR 1875–1900.
   Trinidad-English East Indian Influence.
   Ht.37" W.20" D.32"
   Ebony Wood, with carved back posts, finials and decorative carved crest.
   Shaped upholstered seat, arms and legs.

CENTRE TABLE 1800–1825.
   Barbados-English Influence.
   Ht.27¾" W.34"
   Mahogany, turned pedestal with broken reeded sabre leg tripod, ending in brass lions paws. Round with moulded edge, tip-top feature and original hardware.

DETAIL of carved back of Dining Chair showing gadrooning, scrolls and leaf designs

DINING CHAIR (Pair) 1825–1845.
   Barbados or Martinique-English Influence.
   Ht.35" W.18½" D.17½"
   Mahogany, carved and gadrooned top rail with scroll and leaf motif.
   Centre rail is pierced with similar motifs, caned seat and turned legs.

INTERIOR BEDROOM
Mahogany four-poster bed, dresser and bedside table from St Thomas, *c.* 1830.

DUMB WAITER/TROLLEY 1850–1875.
Barbados-English Influence.
Ht.52" W.48" D.17¾"
Mahogany with three shaped and moulded shelves, supported by carved and pierced sides, on a pair of shaped platforms with turned feet and brass cup toes and castors. The design of the supports have a Gothic flair.
Collection: Russell Prendergast.

SECRETAIRE/DESK 1775–1800.
Barbados-English Chippendale Influence.
Ht.83½" W.37¾" D.22"
Mahogany and Cedar with pull out fall-front drawer, fitted desk interior with drawers and pigeon holes, four drawers below. Upper case with shelves and glass doors of astragal design, with dental moulded cornice. Original brass handles and mechanics thoughout.
(Important)

DETAIL of back of Boudoir Chair with carved and shaped splat of flowers and flower motif on top rail.

DINING CHAIR (Set of six) 1800–1825.
Trinidad or Barbados-English Influence.
Ht.34" W.18" D.16"
Mahogany, simple scrolled top rail, shaped centre rail, caned seat and finished with sabre legs. (Important)

BOUDOIR CHAIR 1850–1875.
St Thomas-French Influence.
Ht.32" W.16" D.15"
Mahogany, shaped open back with carved roses on the top and shaped centre rail, shaped cane seat, serpentine apron and cabriole legs.
Collection: Baroness Mary Sturm-Griendl.

TEA TABLE 1850–1875.
Flensberg, Denmark-Port Furniture (note influence on Tea Table, opposite page).
Ht.30" W. 24"
Mahogany, carved and turned pedestal with carved and scrolled tripod, ending in reverse scroll feet. Round top which unscrews for transportation.
Collection: Russell Prendergast.

TEA TABLE 1875–1899.
  St Thomas-Danish Influence.
  Ht. 30" W. 24"
  Mahogany, turned ring and ball column with shaped
  tripod legs ending in reverse scroll design.
  Collection: Russell Prendergast.

SEWING TABLE 1875–1900.
  Trinidad-English 'Sheraton' Influence.
  Ht.28" W.31"(open) D.16½"
  Mahogany, Satinwood, Ebony and Cedar.
  Mahogany veneer with Satinwood and
  Ebony string inlay design on top and
  sides. Top opens to reveal a silk interior
  with leather pockets, secret drawer opens
  by hidden press.
  Square, tapered legs ending in square
  clubs. Attributed to Kacal's, Port of
  Spain, Trinidad.

HAMMOCK-PLANTER'S CHAIR 1875–1900.
Trinidad/English Arawak Influence.
Ht.30¾" W.25" D.46¼" (open 71½")
Cedar, with turned legs and arm rests, shaped scrolled back, with swing-out arms and canvas covering.

TOWEL RAIL 1800–1825.
St Thomas-Danish Influence.
Ht.28¾" W.24½" D.12"
Mahogany, with simple uprights and bracket feet and rails, arched top and turned throughout.

OBLONG CENTRE TABLE 1875–1889.
Trinidad or Martinique-French Influence.
Ht.29¾" W.27½" D.19"
Cyp, with Walnut veneer decorative motifs. Turned and reeded legs and shaped cross-stretcher, with turned centre finial. Shaped apron with raised Walnut veneered motifs. Incised decoration on apron legs and stretcher. (Renaissance Revival, Important)

120

TOWEL RAIL 1825–1850.
   Trinidad or Barbados-English Influence.
   Ht.29½" W.23½" D.11"
   Cedar, with ball and urn turned uprights, arched top,
   turned rails and leg supports.

CANDLESTAND 1875–1910.
   St Thomas-Danish Influence.
   Ht.28¾" W.22½" D.15½"
   Mahogany, with urn, ring and ball turned pedestal, shaped
   tripod and ending in reverse scroll feet. Serpentine-shaped
   oblong top with shaped and ball-fringed apron.

CANDLESTAND
1875–1890.
   St Thomas-Danish
   Influence.
   Ht.29" W.23" D.16½"
   Mahogany, with urn,
   ball and ring turned
   pedestal and simple
   cabriole tripod, ending
   in scrolled toes. Chamfered rectangular top.

**BUTLER'S TRAY AND
STAND** 1800–1825.
   St Thomas-Danish
   Influence.
   Ht.32¾" W.30¾" D.20"
   Mahogany, with simple
   cross-frame supporting
   tray with raised sides,
   and shaped back and
   cut out handles on the
   sides. Webbing on top
   of cross-frame.

ROCKING CHAIR 1875–1899.
St Thomas-French Influence.
Ht.38" W.23¼" D.33"
Mahogany, Pine, Samann, Thibet, Red Oak, White
Oak and Crappo.
Louis XVI revival featuring carved leaf and scrolled
motif, oval inserted back, supported by scrolled
stretcher, with shaped and scrolled arms, ending in
turned supports with finials. Round caned seat, and
shaped apron, turned front legs and stretchers.
Note: this piece was stained with strong tea to get an
even-looking Mahogany finish, then French
polished. (Important)

CANDLESTAND 1875–1900.
St Thomas-Danish Influence.
Ht.29¾" W.21" D.13¾"
Mahogany, with urn, ring and ball-turned pedestal,
shaped tripod ending in reverse scroll feet.
Serpentine top with shaped, cut-out apron (see
Nos.55, 56).

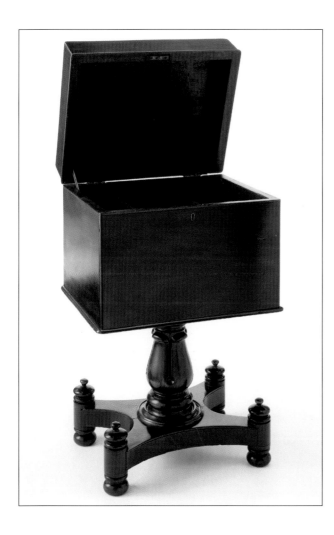

WINE CELLARET 1825–1850.
Barbados-English Influence.
Ht.30" W.18" D.14"
Mahogany, Mahogany veneer, Cedar and Pine. Carved tulip-shaped pedestal, with ring turnings on a shaped base, supported by four turned feet surmounted by finials. The pedestal supports a covered rectangular box with fitted interior.

DRESSING TABLE 1875–1899.
David Peter Corbière of St Thomas
Saint Thomas-Danish Influence.
Mahogany, mahogany veneers with turned supports for oblong-framed mirror, carved crested top, sitting on top of a drawer base. This is on a chest of drawers with split-turned balusters on cantered corners ending with turned feet.
Collection: Enez Harvey.

SLEIGH BED 1850–1875.
   Martinique/Saint Thomas-French Influence.
   Mahogany, with solid scrolled shaped ends on oblong moulded plinth-style feet.
   Collection: Enez Harvey.

SETTEE 1825–1850.
Barbados-English Influence.
Ht.35" W.92" D.24"
Mahogany with carved leaf scroll and gadrooned crest on curved back, meeting with the Greek ionic capital detail of the arm rest. The arms curve down to a reeded seat detail and reeded and turned legs, ending in brass cup castors. (Important)

SMALL TABLE 1875–1899.
Trinidad-French Empire Revival.
Ht. 30¼" D.12"
Mahogany, Cyp with turned legs and stretcher shelf and round top.
Gilded brass mounts, from France.

STOOL 1930-Art Deco.
Ht.18½" W.21" D.15¼"
Mahogany with oval drop-in seat on four simple cabriole legs.

FALL FRONT DESK 1775–1799.

Barbados-English Influence.

Mahogany, with fall front exposing a fitted interior, and a cabinet with single panelled doors below on bracket feet, with brass pineapple motif pulls.

A PAIR OF CAMPAIGN FOLDING CHAIRS
*c.*1875.
  Barbados.
  Mahogany with canvas seats and caned back
  panel.

INTERIOR.

Barbados queen-size four-poster bed with carved leaf, reeded and turned posts. Shaped and carved back with moulded and carved crown and tester. In front of the bed is a chaise-longue with carved back and scrolled arm with turned legs. Caned back, seat and arm, this piece is also from Barbados and is *circa* 1845. Mirrored armoire in the background is from Curaçao, *circa* 1890.

GARDEN PARTY SETTING.

A Bajan caned chaise-longue, canterbury and a Saint Thomian French-Influenced chair in a tropical setting.

SETTEE 1930-Art Deco.
Barbados-English Influence.
Ht.28½" W.45½" D.33" (see also page 108)

DINING TABLE 1800–1825.
Trinidad/Barbados-English Influence.
Ht.29¼" W.58½" D.47½"
Mahogany, with turned urn and ring design pedestal, with four reeded sabre legs and ending in four square brass toes and castors. This table with a stationary top forms the centre part of a set of three to form a banqueting table. The two ends are tip-tops and were moved to the side of the room when not needed. This ensemble was originally part of Government House in Trinidad. (Important)

BLANKET RACK 1800–1825.
Barbados-English Influence.
Ht.59¼" W.52½" D.10"
Mahogany with finely turned supports, finials and three rails on shaped feet. (Important)

BLANKET RACK 1875–1899.
Trinidad-English Influence.
Ht.62" W.47¾" D.12"
Douglas Fir with turned supports, finials and three rails on shaped feet.

BLANKET RACK 1825–1850.
Barbados-English Influence.
Ht.55½" W.56¼" D.15"
Mahogany, with turned supports, finials and two rails on turned and carved feet.

BENCH 1825–1850.
Barbados-English Influence.
Ht.19¾" W.36¾" D.16¼"
Mahogany, carved 'X' framed feet with scrolled toes and turned stretcher. Drop-in upholstered seat.

ETAGERE 1850–1875.
Barbados-English Influence.
Ht.65" W.49" D.13"
Mahogany/Cedar, turned supports and finials with six cedar shelves and edged with reeded mahogany.

131

BOOK SHELVES 1875–1900.
  Barbados-English Influence.
  Ht.56¾" W.48" D.14"
  Mahogany/Cedar with five shelves in waterfall design
  connected with turned supports and ending in bun feet.

HALLWAY. MIRROR CONSOLE of the Art Nouveau
period, around 1900.
  Mahogany with mirrored top and console.

BOOK SHELVES 1875–1900.
  Barbados-English Influence.
  Ht.60" W.42" D.13"
  Mahogany/Cedar, six shelves with scrolled cut-out design
  supports and top, with ball feet.

BREAKFAST TABLE 1800–1825.
Barbados-English Influence.
Ht.31" D.43¼"
Mahogany with turned pedestal tripod
and broken sabre legs. Reeded shoulder
on legs ending in brass claws and castors.
(Important)

CORNER ETAGERE 1875–1899.
Saint Thomas-French Influence.
Ht.67" W.27¼" D.17"
Mahogany with turned supports and
finials, five shelves with shaped and
moulded side rails, serpentine front,
and pierced carved and shaped top.

SIDEBOARD 1875–1899.
Saint Thomas-Danish Influence.
Ht.58" W.39" D.22⅜"
Mahogany with turned supports and legs and three shelves.
Mirrored and shelved top. This form of sideboard is descended
from the seventeenth century English court cupboard.

SUTHERLAND GATELEG TABLE 1875–1900.
  Trinidad/Barbados-English (Sheraton revival).
  Ht.22" W.22¼" D.51/2" (open 25⅜")
Mahogany, mahogany veneer, Cedar, Satinwood, Ebony and
Green Heart, with six turned legs. Mahogany veneer on cedar
top with inlaid cross-banding of Ebony and Satinwood on top
edge. Centre motif inlaid with Ebony, Satinwood and Green
heart. Legs are made of Cedar.

DRAWING ROOM.
    EARLY 19TH CENTURY COLLAPSIBLE ARMOIRE from Flensberg or St. Croix in the neo-classical style, flattened pilasters and arched details. In the foreground, a marble-topped mahogany parlour table, shaped apron with drops and carved and reeded pedestal tripod, St Thomas, 1850.

BEDROOM CORNER.
  FRENCH ANTILLES COURBARIL ARMOIRE of the Louis XVI period *circa* 1780.
  This piece is restrained and elegant with mahogany panels.

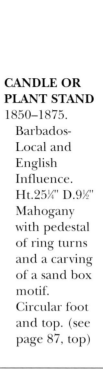

**CANDLE OR
PLANT STAND**
1850–1875.
Barbados-
Local and
English
Influence.
Ht.25¼" D.9½"
Mahogany
with pedestal
of ring turns
and a carving
of a sand box
motif.
Circular foot
and top. (see
page 87, top)

STOOL 1750–1775.
Barbados-English Chippendale Influence.
Ht.13" W.26½" D.22"
Mahogany and Cedar with carved cabriole legs, leaf knees and scrolled toes.
Upholstered top. (Important)

CHEST 1775–1799.
Trinidad/Barbados-English Influence (Bermuda?).
Ht.19¼" W.29½" D.20¾"
Cedar with shaped feet and apron supporting a dovetailed
box with moulded top. Brass handles.

VANITY 1875–1899.
Saint Thomas-Danish Influence.
Ht.27" W.19" D.11"
Mahogany with shaped top over single drawer. Two ball, ring
and urn turned uprights, holding mahogany-framed oblong
mirror.

RECLINING ARMCHAIR

1825–1850.

Barbados-English Influence.
Ht.38" W.25" D.27" (extension 33")

Mahogany with carved scrolled arm and supports on turned and reeded legs. Upholstered seat and back. Ratchet pulls make the arms extend to allow the back to recline, with pull-out foot rest. This is a rare mechanical piece.

Provenance: Part of the original furnishings of Sam Lord's Castle, Barbados, built c.1830. Containing tag from the 'Institute of Culture', to allow for exportation. (Important)

INTERIOR, with mahogany pedestal sideboard from St Thomas or Curaçao, with carved palm design on back splash, four drawers with crystal pulls (crystal pulls were used extensively in Curaçao), above two cupboards on turned ball feet, *circa* 1870. Collection: Corrine Lockhart.

INTERIOR, showing large mahogany cabinet with broken pediment, urn centre above glass doors. The bottom half has a two door cabinet with barley twist columns on corners, three drawers with wooden handles and ending in turned feet. This piece was made by St Thomas cabinetmaker Fred Essanason, *circa* 1925.
Collection: Corrine Lockhart.

SMALL HALL CHAIR 1850–1875.
Barbados/Trinidad-English Influence.
Ht.34" W.17½" D.14"
Mahogany with carved and pierced lyre-shaped back, shaped and moulded seat with turned legs.

DETAIL of Centre Table with carved and punched leaf motif.

CENTRE TABLE 1850–1875.
Trinidad/Martinique-Louis XV revival.
Ht.28" W.35½" D.17¼"
Cedar with turned supports and stretcher on carved and shaped legs.

DETAIL of Chaise-Longue showing carved and scrolled arms and legs and profile of the back.

CHAISE-LONGUE 1850–1875.
Trinidad/Martinique-Louis XV revival.
Ht.35½" W.31½" D.73½"
Mahogany with six carved and scrolled legs, supported by turned stretchers with carved and scrolled arm supports, double caned arms and single caned back. Upholstered seat. (Important)

143

HALF ROUND TABLE (One of a pair) 1825–1850.
Saint Thomas-Danish Influence.
Ht.30" W.56" D.27½"
Bullet Wood with turned legs ending in brass cup toes and castors. Apron is cross-banded with Bullet Wood veneer on solid Bullet Wood. (Important)

WASH STAND 1850–1875.
Saint Thomas-Danish Influence.
Ht.36" W.23" D.17½"
Mahogany with turned urn, ball and ring legs and supports. Shaped skirting on drawer and apron with spindle gallery and shaped back. Cut-out in top for basin. Towel rails on side.
Collection: Felipe Ayala.

WASH STAND 1850–1875.
Saint Thomas-Danish Influence.
Ht.36½" W.21¾" D.17"
Mahogany with turned urn, ball and ring legs and supports, lower drawer, top with spindled gallery and carved back-splash, top with cut-out for the basin.
Collection: Gwendolyn Kean.

144

UNIVERSAL TABLE (gatelegged) 1750–1775.
  Barbados-English Influence.
  Ht.29½" W.30½" D.16¾"
  Mahogany with straight chamfered legs with incised lines carved on front legs. Folded
  top with gate leg for support when open.

LIBRARY TABLE 1825–1850.
  Barbados-English Influence.
  Ht.30" W.57¼" D.27"
  Mahogany, mahogany veneer. Pine with two reeded and turned legs
  on platform, ending with carved feet. Top cross-banded with flame
  mahogany and panelled sides and ends also in flame mahogany. This
  piece is important because it carries a rare maker's label from
  Barbados which reads as follows: '—— Sharton, cabinetmakers and
  upholsterers. Swan Street, Bridgetown, B——.'

WAGONETTE OR SIDEBOARD 1850–1875.
  Saint Croix-Danish Influence.
  Ht.50¼" W.47½" D.23"
  Mahogany with turned legs, supports and finials, with three galleried shelves and brass cup castors. This piece is the descendant of the medieval court cupboard.

CONSOLE TABLE 1825–1850.
  Barbados-English Influence.
  Ht.34½" W.32½" D.19"
  Mahogany, mahogany veneer. Cedar with elaborately carved cabriole front legs with leaf and scroll motif on knees ending with paw feet. Back legs are turned and supported by a shaped platform on bun feet.
  The top with a drawer is cross-banded in mahogany with a shaped panel veneered in flame mahogany. (Important)

LIBRARY TABLE 1800–1825.
  Barbados-English Influence.
  Ht.30" W.49" D.29"
  Mahogany with turned and reeded legs ending in brass cup toes
  and castors. Three long drawers with wooden knobs in top.

DINING TABLE 1800–1825.
  Barbados-English Influence.
  Ht.29" D.54"
  Mahogany with turned urn-shaped
pedestal on four splayed, reeded legs
ending with brass claw toes. Round top
with cross-banded apron.

SOFA TABLE 1800–1825.
Barbados-Sheraton Influence.
Ht.28⅛" W.33⅛" D.25⅛"
Mahogany, Satinwood, Baleen and
Cedar with drop leaves and two
drawers with two opposite dummies.
Turned stretcher, lyre-shaped
support on broken sabre legs
ending in brass paw feet. All the
inlay is on solid Mahogany.
(Important)

DINING TABLE 1800–1825.
  Trinidad-Louis XVI Influence.
  Ht.30" W.60"
  Green Heart, round, when open, with six square tapered gatelegs
  ending in club toes. Round top with moulded edge, and drop leaves.
  Collection: Baroness Mary Greindl.

STAND 1875–1900.
  Flensberg, Denmark-German Influence.
  Ht.36½" D.12⅜"
  Oak with spiral-turned support, round top,
  round base on four carved 'goat hoof' toes.
  Collection: Gwendolyn Kean.

CHEST OF DRAWERS 1825–1850.
  Barbados-English Influence.
  Ht.40" W.47½" D.21⅜"
  Mahogany, mahogany veneer and Cedar, with four drawers. Top drawer
  designed to be three drawers but is one drawer, cross-banding on all
  drawers with wooden knobs. Reeded and turned inserted columns on
  corners and ending in turned feet. Shaped back detail.

PEMBROKE TABLE
1775–1799.
  Barbados-English Influence.
Ht.29¾" W.32½" D.20½"
Mahogany, Red Oak and
Baleen with slender, turned
legs ending in brass cup toe
castors. Drop leaves with
butterfly supports, with
inlaid drawer. Ebony edging
and wooden knob. Invented
by the Earl of Pembroke as a
dining table to accommodate
small intimate groups
(Important)

CHAISE-LONGUE 1825–1850.
Barbados-English Influence.
Ht.23" W.71½" D.21"
Mahogany with carved and
scrolled arm and back with
turned legs ending in brass
toes with ball castors. Caned seat,
side and back.

CHAISE-LONGUE 1825–1850.
Trinidad/Martinique-French
Influence.
Ht.33" W.77" D.22¼"
Mahogany with carved and
scrolled leaf motif on arm and
back with turned legs ending in
brass cup toes and with porcelain
castors. Caned seat, back and
side.

CHAISE-LONGUE 1825–1850.
Barbados-English Influence.
Ht.31" W.77" D.22"
Mahogany with carved and
scrolled leaf motif on arm and
back with turned legs, ending in
brass cup toes and porcelain
castors. Caned seat back and side
(similar to smaller example, top
of page).

ARMOIRE 1800–1825.
St. Thomas/Martinique/Louis XV Influence.
Ht.72" W.54" D.19"
This armoire, which is very similar to the example on page 173, is made from Courbaril, Lemonwood and Walnut. The Courbaril doors with shaped frames enclose two panels each of West Indian Walnut. With a moulded, shaped and rounded-corner removable cornice. It also has a shaped apron on the front, bottom and sides ending in cabriole legs with hoofed toes. It has three panels on each side made of Lemonwood. Brass fiche/barrel hinges and escutcheons. (Maybe a trade import from New Orleans.)

PARTNERS' KNEEHOLE DESK 1775–1800.
Barbados-English/Sheraton Influence.
Ht.31¼" W.42" D.27¼"
Mahogany, Mahogany Veneer, Cedar, Satinwood. This desk is veneered with Mahogany over Cedar. The top, sides, legs and drawers are inlaid with Satinwood in a string design. Both front and back have the same design of four drawers and a cupboard, the drawers have wooden handles. The kneehole has a shaped design on four tapered legs with brass castors. (Important)

INTERIOR, showing a pair of plant stands with a zoomorphic design of snakes around a turned centre pedestal with tripod stand. Round tops with shaped aprons, St Thomas, *circa* 1880. Mahogany.
Collection: Corrine Lockhart.

CABINET 1775–1800.

Martinique-Louis XV Influence.

Ht.43½" W.45" D.17"

Rosewood and Mahogany with inserted marble in moulded top, serpentine-shaped front and sides, with carved shell and flower motif on front. Two doors with carved wooden escutcheons, shaped base and apron ending in cabriole feet with carved scroll motif. (Important)

ARMCHAIR 1850–1875.

Trinidad/Martinique – French Empire Revival Influence.

Ht.37¼" W.22" D.20½"

Crapaud Wood with gilded mounts imported from France, square upholstered back and seat, with arms on tapering square-shaped legs ending in brass paw feet. Top rail rolls back with gilded mounts.

CARD TABLE 1750–1775.

Barbados-English Chippendale Influence.

Ht.28⅜" W.32½" D.15¾" Open:32⅜" x 31½"

Mahogany, Cedar and Pine with cabriole legs, carved leaf knees and club toes. Shaped top with beaded decoration and veneered apron, top opens by swivel action. Green baize interior. (Important)

CHEST OF DRAWERS 1750–1775.
Barbados-English Chippendale
Influence.
Ht.41" W.41¼" D.21"
Mahogany and Cedar with a pair of
drawers on top, three lower drawers
with original brass pulls. Carcass in
Cedar with Mahogany top, sides and
front on four bracket feet.

CARD TABLE 1890–1910.
Barbados/Trinidad-English Sheraton Revival.
Ht.30¾" W.19¾" D.19¾" Open: 28⅛" square.
Mahogany, Cedar and Satinwood with square top that is quartered to open after a ninety-degree swivel.
Drawer with brass pulls on four slender legs and brass and porcelain castors.
Satinwood string inlay decoration throughout. Baize interior on top.

MIRROR 1875–1900.
  Barbados-English Influence.
  Ht.30" W.34¼" D.11¾"
  Mahogany with oval bevelled mirror. Shaped and carved open
  stand on shaped bracket feet, shaped cross-bar with two curved
  arms holding the elongated oval framed mirror, brass swivel knobs.

MIRROR 1875–1900.
  Trinidad/Martinique-French Influence.
  Ht.36" W.28½" D.2¾"
  Mahogany with round bevelled mirror, concave-
  shaped, round, beaded and moulded frame with
  carved and applied leaf and scroll motif on the
  top and bottom of the frame.

TABLE 1825–1850.
  Barbados-English Influence.
  Ht.29" W.30" D.16¾"
  Mahogany, mahogany veneer and
  Cedar with rectangular top cross-
  banded apron on two shaped reeded
  and turned legs, on cross supports
  ending with carved and scrolled toes.
  Turned cross-stretcher.

SIDE TABLE 1775–1800.
Martinique-Louis XV Influence.
Ht.32¼" W.49" D.23½"
Courbaril and Mahogany with three drawers, wooden pulls, shaped apron on four cabriole legs, with carved scrolled leaf motif on knees and ending with scrolled toes. (Important)

CONSOLE TABLE 1800–1825.
Trinidad-Louis XV Influence.
Ht.39¼" W.62¼" D.18¾"
Saman with serpentine-shaped top of white marble, shaped apron, with raised carved flower garland design across front, on four cabriole legs with carved flowers and scrolls on knees and ending with scrolled toes. (Important)

SLANT TOP DESK 1875–1900.
Trinidad/Barbados-English Sheraton Revival Influence.
Ht.39" W.35½" D.16"
Mahogany, mahogany veneer, Satinwood and Cedar with inlaid and veneered front flap, with pull-outs for support encasing a fitted interior of Cedar with Satinwood inlay. Three drawers below with inlaid and veneered decorations and original French-style pulls. Bracketed feet and brass gallery around the top.

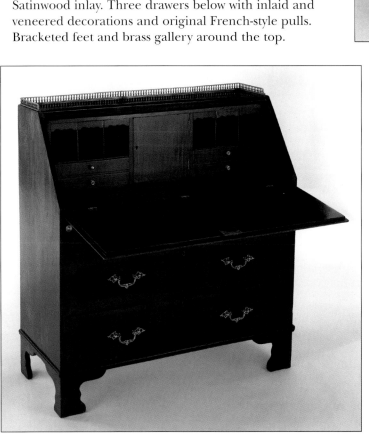

SOFA TABLE 1825–1850.
Barbados-English Influence.
Ht.29¼" W.39¾" D.28"
Mahogany, Cedar and Pine with cross-banded edge on top and two drawers with wooden knobs and false drawer fronts on opposite side. Carved scroll motif, butterfly supports for drop leaf ends. Reeded and turned centre support on shaped platform supported by four feet carved from the 'sand box fruit' design.

PRINT.
Depiction of the Sand Box Tree found in Barbados. This motif is found on Barbados furniture and the tree grows throughout the Lesser Antilles. English, *circa* 1780.

GENTLEMAN'S WARDROBE 1775–1800.
Barbados-English Influence.
Ht.83" W.48" D.24"
Mahogany and Cedar with two-door cabinet above and chest with three drawers below, all are made as one unit. Rectangular moulded panelled doors and wooden drawer knobs on a platform-style base. Simple, shaped cornice and interior slide-out shelving.

SMALL ARMOIRE 1775–1800.
Trinidad/Martinique-Louis XV Influence.
Ht.55" W.43" D.18"
Purple Heart with two doors with shaped panels and brass fiche/barrel hinges. Two panels on each side with shaped side and front aprons on cabriole legs ending in scrolled toes on hoofs. Detachable moulded cornice on top. (Important)

SIDEBOARD 1825–1850.
Barbados-English Influence.
Mahogany, Cedar and Pine with two pedestals with drawers
and single door cabinet with moulded tops. Two drawers in
the projecting centre part with cross-banding on all the
drawers and doors. Twist turned corner posts on lower
cabinets, on top of a platform with bun feet. The back splash
is shaped and carved with a sunburst motif. Carved wooden
handles. Collection: Margaret Creque.

LIBRARY TABLE 1825–1850.
Barbados-English Influence.
Ht.29" W.48½" D.41½"
Mahogany, Cedar and Pine, double-sided with two long
drawers and two false drawer fronts on opposite side,
wooden pulls. Unique carved leaf, scroll and branch
motif supports standing on narrow platforms and
ending on scroll feet. Turned X-frame stretchers and
two carved and tulip motif cross-stretchers.
Custom made for Buckley Plantation in Barbados about
1835. (Unique and Important.)

SIDEBOARD 1825–1850.
St Croix-Danish Influence.
Ht.54⅛" W.41⅛" D.22¼"
Mahogany with four turned legs, supporting two concave
centre drawers and two side-cupboards with spindle
railing and scroll ends, along the top of the cupboards
from back to front. Shaped back with mirror inset and
shelves.

CHEST ON CHEST 1775–1800.
Barbados-English/Chippendale Influence.
Ht.69½" W.43" D.21¾"
Mahogany and Cedar with Mahogany veneer on a Cedar carcass, in two parts. The top has two small and three large drawers with simple moulded cornice. The bottom has three large drawers, the whole on four bracket feet. The original brassware was imported from England.

SOFA 1825–1850.
Barbados-English late Regency Influence.
Ht.38½" W.96" D.28"
Mahogany with Cedar carcass. Upholstered with a shaped back and carved fern tendrils motif on the crest. Scrolled arms with carved scroll motifs, on four turned and reeded legs with brass toes and ball castors.

HAT STAND
1875–1899.
St. Thomas-Danish Influence.
Ht.73¾" W.17½"
Mahogany, with brass and porcelain hangers. A turned ball, ring and shaped stand on a carved and shaped tripod base, ending in inverted scroll toes with brass castors.

STANDING SCREEN (Set of three) 1900–1925. Art Nouveau. Trinidad-English and Indian Influence.
Ht.86¾" W.45" D.15" (large screen); Ht.86¾" W.24" D.15" (small pair)
Rosewood with moulded and panelled bottom and centre with louvered top, crowned with a filigree carved and pierced tiara. This filigree is reminiscent of the jewellery brought to Trinidad by the East Indians in the 1840s and onwards. These screens were part of the original furnishings of Stollmeyer's Castle in Port of Spain, Trinidad.

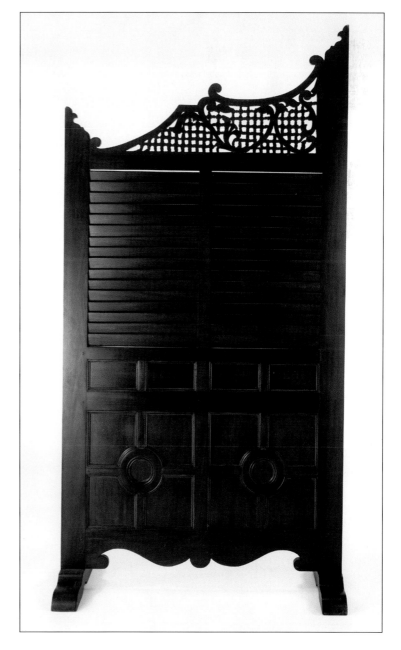

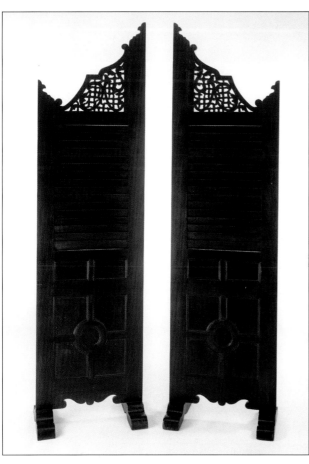

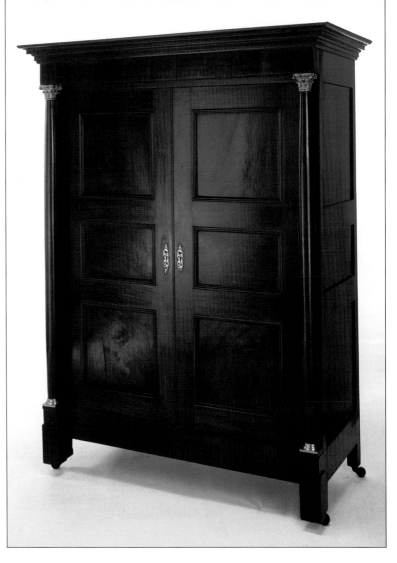

CHINA CABINET 1800–1825.
Barbados-Sheraton Influence.
Ht.83" W.43" D.18½"
Mahogany with Cedar lined interiors. In two pieces, the top part is set back with glazed astragal doors, Cedar shelves, and a moulded cornice. The bottom half has two doors and cedar shelving, and top and bottom edges reeded, sitting on four turned legs.

ARMOIRE 1825–1850.
Martinique/Trinidad – French Empire Influence.
Ht.75" W.57" D.26½"
This medium-sized Mahogany Armoire has two doors with three panels each. Close inspection shows these panels are made of two pieces of wood each. This detail has been seen often in French case furniture and is believed to be part of the design. A pair of free-standing columns on either side sit on square plinths, with ormolu capitals and feet on castors. The whole surmounted by a moulded cornice.

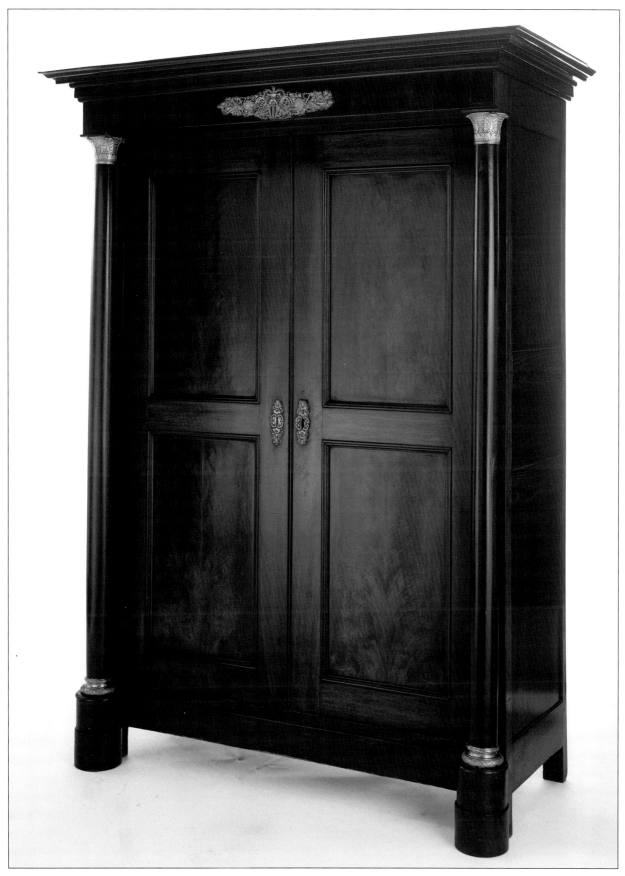

ARMOIRE 1825–1850.

Trinidad/Martinique-French Empire Style.

Ht.82" W.62" D.29½"

Large Mahogany wardrobe with Cedar-lined interior, with two moulded panelled doors in matching figured mahogany. A pair of free-standing columns on large circular plinths, with ormolu capitals and feet. The mounts show an Egyptian influence. The other mounts are of music and armoury motifs, all surmounted by a shaped cornice. (Important)

163

INTERIOR.
  Mahogany armoire from St Thomas with single panel doors of flame Mahogany, with split baluster columns on the sides, of urn, ball and ring turned design. The base stands on square plinth feet, *circa* 1875.

INTERIOR.

Mahogany cabinet with Cedar sub-structure with two flame Mahogany panelled doors, two drawers with wooden knobs. Spirally carved and turned inserted corner posts on a plain raised platform, *circa* 1845. Above this is an American Mahogany and gilded Empire mirror with carved and gilded leaf motifs on the corners. It was originally part of the furnishings of Governor Jurgen Levien Rhode, of the Danish Virgin Islands, 1822–1854. It came out of Crown House, the Governor's residence at that time. *Circa* 1840.

CRIB/CHILD'S BED 1825–1850.

St Thomas/St Croix-Danish Influence.
Ht.75" W.41" D.59"
A pretty Mahogany four-poster bed with slim turned ring, urn and ball posts. Turned, spindled balustrade completely surrounds the bed, with one side able to be lowered for access. The whole is moulded, turned and reeded on brass toes and castors. (Important)

FOUR-POSTER BED 1800–1825.

Barbados-English Sheraton Influence.
Ht.87½" W.42" D.82"
This single Mahogany bed has posts of reeded urns, twist turns and ring turns. The headboard is a simple ram's head design.

FOUR-POSTER BED 1780–1800.

Trinidad/French Influence.
Ht.87½" W.63¾" D.82½"
This bed is made from the dense and heavy Roblewood, Courbaril and has a headboard with a uniquely carved and pierced motif. The carvings on the side of the headboard and the mouldings are applied. The posts are carved with palm leaf motifs and twisted, ring and ball turnings, all on carved leaf motif legs. (Important)

ARMOIRE 1825–1850.

Trinidad/Martinique-French Empire
Influence.

Ht.83½" W.61½" D.27"

This Mahogany wardrobe has two doors
with three panels each. The split panel
motif, mentioned before, is seen here
again. Two free-standing columns with
unusually carved and turned motifs, stand
on square plinths with ormolu capitals and
feet. Ormolu escutcheons and other
mounts are French and original. The
moulded cornice is removable.

ARMOIRE 1875–1900.

Trinidad/Martinique-French Louis XVI
revival.

Ht.104" W.39¼" D.24"

Made from Roblewood (tabebuia) and
Cedar. It has a single door with a bevelled-
shaped mirror and brass escutcheon. A
pair of carved reeded and turned
columns, topped by urn finials are free-
standing on square moulded and carved
plinths. The bottom encloses a drawer
which stands on four turned legs. The
entire piece is surmounted by a bonnet
top, carved and reeded with applied
mouldings of Cedar. On top of this is a
carved leaf and flower motif around a
beaded shield (see detail).

ROCKING CHAIR 1850–1875.
   St Thomas-Danish Influence.
   Ht.37½" W.21" D.29"
   This Mahogany rocking chair has a caned seat
   and back with curved arms on turned supports
   and front legs. It has a turned stretcher in front
   with five other stretchers connecting all the
   legs. The back is shaped, and the top rail is
   curved and pierced to form a handle.

ARMCHAIR (One of a pair) 1825–1850.
   Martinique-French Empire Style.
   Ht.38½" W.23¼" D.31"
   This Mahogany armchair has a drop-in upholstered seat,
   the arms and arm support are in the swan design. Curved
   legs end in paw feet, the back is high with a wide-shaped
   splat, and rolled motif on the top rail. This swan design was
   made famous by Empress Josephine of Martinique in her
   bedroom at the Chateau de Malmaison.
   Collection: Margaret Creque.

FOUR-POSTER BED 1825–1850.

Barbados-English Influence.

Ht.101" W.70" D.81½"

This Mahogany bed has four posts with the carved tulip design, carved leafy urns and turned motifs. The shaped back has a carved medallion of leaves, topped by a rolling- pin design with turned finials. The foot-board is also carved with leaves and scrolls, and the crown and tester has moulded and carved motifs.

CHAISE-LONGUE (Pair) 1825–1850.
  Barbados-English Influence.
  Ht.35" W.65" D.23½" (male)
  Ht.33" W.62½" D.22" (female)
  These mahogany chaises-longues have caned seats, arms, backs and scrolled ends. The arms are shaped and carved with a leaf motif, the back is also shaped with a leaf and scroll motif. The seat is scrolled or turned back in the Grecian style, with turned and carved tulip design legs ending in brass toes and castors. (Important)

ROCKING CHAIR 1850–1875
Barbados-English Influence
Mahogany with upholstered seat, back and arm rests. The arms with carved scroll motifs curve into the sabre legs ending on the gliders. The seat and back shaped in a sinuous curve ending with a roll top on the back.
Collection: Russell Prendergast. ´

TIERED SERVING TABLE
1775–1800.
England-Port Furniture (Gillows and Lancaster). Ht.44" D.27"
Mahogany with three graduated circular shelves that rotate. Supported by a turned centre column on a carved and shaped tripod base, ending in snake head toes. This table unscrews for shipment.

CELLARET 1825–1850.
Barbados-English Influence. Ht.19" W.12" D.12"
Mahogany with Cedar interior, divided into four sections for bottles. The top is carved with a sun-burst motif, with wooden handles and brass carrying handles on the sides. The cellaret stands on four turned legs.

INTERIOR.
View of Mahogany marble-topped console, Trinidad/Martinique, *circa* 1880.
Collection: Adrian Camps-Campins.
Photograph of Adrian Camps-Campins' mother, Louie Camps Campins née Grell on left with her mother
Edith Grell née Gransaull on right, taken on Frederick Street, Port of Spain, Trinidad in 1939.

BEDSIDE TABLE 1850–1875.
Barbados-English Influence.
Ht.35" W.22½" D.14"
This table is taller than usual and is made to sit alongside a high four-poster bed. It is made from Mahogany with turned legs and supports. It has a middle shelf with three drawers and wooden handles. The top has a shaped apron.

ARMOIRE 1800–1825.
Trinidad/Martinique-Louis XV Influence.
Ht.70" W.47½" D.20½"
This small armoire is made of Mahogany, Courbaril and West Indian Walnut. The shaped door frames are made from Courbaril enclosing panels of Walnut. It has a moulded, shaped and rounded-corner cornice and two mahogany panels on each side. It stands on shaped cabriole legs and ends in scrolled toes with a shape apron on the bottom, front and sides. It has brass fiche/barrel hinges and escutcheons.
(Important)

STUMP POST BED *c.*1840. A rare pair.
Barbados.
Mahogany, with turned posts and carved and turned rolling-pin headboard.

Oil painting of the author's mother Dorothy, displayed in its usual position in the family home

MAHOGANY DIAMOND AND HEART-SHAPED COCKTAIL TABLES
22in. high. Trinidad, *c.*1940

CUPPING/RUM TABLE 1850–1875.
St Thomas/St Croix-Danish Influence.
Ht.45½" W.34½" D.22"
This side table is made from Thibet wood with a Pine sub-structure. The front drawer with wooden handles has a scalloped-designed bottom which carries throughout the sides. The legs have turned ball, ring, and urn designs. The top has a spindled gallery and shaped cut-out and mirrored back. These tables sometimes came in pairs or fours and were distributed in the public rooms.

PEDESTAL SIDEBOARD 1800–1825.
Barbados-English Influence.
Ht.44" W.72" D.18¼"
This sideboard is made of Mahogany with a mixed Pine and Cedar sub-structure. The panels on the cupboard doors are in the shape of an Egyptian plinth showing the influence of the Egyptian style after Napoleon's campaigns. The plinths sit on the top of carved gadrooning. The drawers of the pedestals above the cupboards and the protruding centre part have beaded surrounds. The tops of the cupboards have an inward-curved platform. This piece comes apart in three sections and everything sits on eight turned feet. (Important)

BEACH SCENE.
  Showing an Empire Revival nineteenth century Trinidadian armchair and side table, with a Planters Punch drink.

ROCKER ON A ROCK.
 Saint Thomas, early nineteenth century rocker, on a rock
 by the Caribbean Sea.

Appendix 1
English and French Periods
Rulers and Dates

APPENDIX 2
DATE TABLE OF ENGLISH AND FRENCH STYLES

ENGLISH STYLES

DATE	KING OR QUEEN	STYLE
1660	Charles II	French Influence/Antique Baroque.
1685	James II	Heavy 'S' & 'C' Scrolls/Foliage.
1689	William III & Mary II	Sea and Water motifs, Marquetry inlay and gilded mounts.
1702	Anne	Exotic influence, cabriole legs, japanning.
1714	George I	Walnut veneer, introduction of mahogany.
1727	George II	Dark woods, claw and ball feet. Rococo, gothic and Chinese influence. Chippendale-style era.
1760	George III	Neo-Classical Greek, Roman, influences, light-coloured woods and inlays, and fine straight lines. Sheraton/Hepplewhite-style era.
1820	George IV	Egyptian, Greek, and Asian influences. Solid and exotic woods or gilt mounts or brass and precious material inlays. Regency-style era.
1830	William IV	Heavier influences of previous styles, a lot of carving, and less gilding. Late Regency-style era.
1837	Victoria	Revival of all the periods, from Elizabeth I, to George IV. Involving carving, inlaying, veneering, gilding, etc. Arts and Crafts Movement. Victorian-style era.
1901	Edward VII	Sheraton and Hepplewhite revival, and the introduction of Art Nouveau using plant and nature motifs.
1910	George V	Continuation of Art Nouveau, and previous styles. Also introduction to Art Deco, *circa* 1928 to 1939.

FRENCH STYLES

DATE	KING OR QUEEN	STYLE
1643	Louis XIV	Baroque, gilded brass, precious inlays and exotic woods. Emphasis on gilded decorations.
1715	Louis XV	Light woods, marquetry and parquetry in mahogany, and other precious hard woods. Rococo and 'S' and 'C' scrolls, gilded mounts, and Asian influences.
1774	Louis XVI	Neo-Classicism, straight lines, Pompeiian and Greek influences, and minimal gilded mounts on solid mahogany.
1795	Directoire Consulate	Simplistic Louis XVI-style, straight lines, solid mahogany, few gilded mounts.
1799	Napoleon I Napoleon II	Empire-style, Egyptian, Roman, Greek and African, influences. Solid mahogany and other solid woods. Re-emergence of gilded mounts.
1814	Louis XVIII Charles X	Restoration-style, Late Empire with heavy carving, light and dark woods without mounts.
1830	Louis-Philippe	Dark Mahogany with simple lines, no mounts, but with mouldings and little carving.
1848	Louis Napoleon Bonaparte	Revival of the Louis XIV-, XV-, XVI- styles, exaggerated bronzes and Asian motifs.
1852	Napoleon III	Revival period of all previous styles, with exaggeration.

Napoleon III was deposed in 1870, when France became a republic. The revival of previous styles continued, using inferior materials, bringing about the Art Nouveau Movement in the 1900s with a revival of exotic woods, inlays, and bronzes, in natural shapes. Art Moderne, with its technical style, and straight lines, appeared in 1928, a reaction to the Art Nouveau Movement.

Appendix 3
Furniture Labels

There is little known information about the cabinetmakers, as far as their lives or workplaces are concerned, and few surviving labels from their pieces that had been labelled. Even the large collection featured in this volume contains only three examples. Items of furniture with these rare labels serve as a cornerstone to identifying other pieces.

St Croix has records of several artisans; such as Charles MacFarlan, of the nineteenth century and Peter Thurland of the twentieth century. St Thomas records Mr Esaanason, and Edgar Steele, also of the nineteenth and twentieth centuries. Barbados has a Mr Sharton and Bryant & Sons of the nineteenth century and Curaçao has a number of recorded nineteenth century artisans, including the famed William Chapman and Gerard de Windt.

Four pieces in this collection contain labels: The first, a wardrobe of the Art Nouveau (c.1900) period, from Curaçao by J. E. Pierre, has three labels inside. I believe the label is in three different languages: Dutch? Spanish? Papiemento?

> 'Ebanisteria La Elegancia'
> J. E. Pierre
> Centir Steeg no. 201 Otrabanda,
> Curazao.
> Este Establecimiento se en Cuentre
> Constanoeate un Varaido Surtido
> De Muebles
> Se Hace Ademas A Precib Modico
> Con Breredad Elegancia
> Cualquier Trabajo Del Ramo
> Buen Gusta-Modicidad-Ageo

The second piece is a late Regency (1840s) mahogany library table from Barbados by Mr Sharton, the remains of the label reads:

> ....Sharton
> Cabinet makers and
> Upholsterers
> Swan street Bridgetown
> B...................................

LIBRARY TABLE 1825–1850.
Barbados-English Influence.
Ht.30" W.57¼" D.27"
Mahogany, mahogany veneer. Pine with two reeded and turned legs on platform, ending with carved feet. Top cross-banded with flame mahogany and panelled sides and ends also in flame mahogany. This piece is important because it carries a rare maker's label from Barbados which reads as follows: '—— Sharton, cabinetmakers and upholsterers. Swan Street, Bridgetown, B——.'

The third piece is a pair of mahogany rockers from (1900–1925), Barbados by C. F. Harrison, the label reads:

Manufactured by
C. F. Harrison & Co. Ltd.
Barbados W.I.

The fourth piece is a slant-front desk and is illustrated below with details of the maker's label.

Lady's Slant-Front Desk
Mahogany with cedar carcass and interior.
Barbados, circa 1920.
49in. x 28in. x 16in.

The maker's label on the back reads:

'Manufactured by C. F. Harrison & Co. Ltd.
in Barbados.'

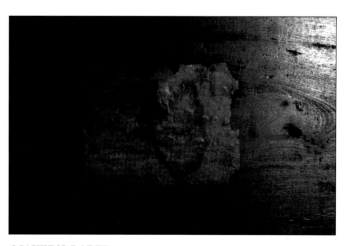

MAKER'S LABEL.
Depiction of Maker's Label on Armoire (see page 57).

BIBLIOGRAPHY

A Sketch Map History of the Caribbean, Robert Greenland. 1991

Hand Book of Kings and Queens, 'Wordsworth' John E. Morby. 1989

A Brief History of the Caribbean, Jan Rogozinski. 1994

Great English Furniture, 'Malletts' Lanto Synge. 1991

Timbers of Tropical America, 'Record', Yale University Press. 1924

The Connoisseur Complete Encyclopedia of Antiques, Peerage Press. 1975

The Dictionary of English Furniture, Ralph Edwards. 1924

Bois-Essences et Variétés, Jean Giullano. Editions H. Vial. 1996

World Woods in Color, William A. Lincoln. 1996

L'Art Mobilier De La Martinique Aux XVIII et XIX Siècles, Département De La Martinique Office National Des Forêts par Françoise Darmezin de Garlande et Joseph Poupon. 1923

Caribbean Style, Slesin, Cliff, Berthelot, Gaume, Rozensztroch. 1985

Maisons de Martinique, Brigitte Marry et Roland Suvelor. Foundation Clement, Arthaud. 1996

Treasures of Barbados, Henry S. Fraser. 1990

Scientific Sorties, Anthony De Verteuil. 1993

Profile Trinidad, Michael Anthony. 1975

'Barbados', Encyclopaedia Britannica Online (accessed March 14, 1999)

A Traveller's Guide to Caribbean History, James Ferguson. 1997

'Grenada', Encyclopaedia Britannica Online (accessed March 14, 1999)

General History of the Caribbean, Franklin W. Knight. 1997

Le Meuble de Port, Louis Malfoy. 1992

'*Martinique*', Encyclopaedia Britannica Online (accessed March 14, 1999)

'*Netherland Antilles*', Encyclopaedia Britannica Online (accessed March 14, 1999)

The Lesser Antilles In The Age Of European Expansion, University Press of Gainsville. 1996

A Short History Of The West Indies, J. H. Parry. 1987

'*Trinidad and Tobago*', Encyclopaedia Britannica Online (accessed March 14, 1999)

'*Virgin Islands*', Encyclopaedia Britannica Online (accessed March 14, 1999)

Leaflets From The Danish West Indies, Dr Charles E. Taylor. 1887

GLOSSARY

Acanthus The leaf used in classical design, adapted as a furniture motif, especially by Chippendale, on the knees of cabriole legs.

Armoire French word for large wardrobe.

Bajan A derivation of Barbadian to Barbajan to Bajan.

Baleen A horny substance attached in plates to the upper jaw of the Baleen whales, used to filter krill.

Ball Foot A spherical foot.

Barley Sugar A twisted/turning design on the sides or backs of chairs and on the sides of wardrobes.

Baroque A French term meaning whimsical, grotesque and irregularly-shaped.

Bas-Relief A sculptural projection.

Bead and Reel A moulding of round and oblong combinations.

Bedstead A piece of furniture for sleeping.

Bed Steps The stairs used to access high four-poster beds. (West Indian)

Bell Flower Hanging flower bud of three to five petals, carved or inlaid, sometimes designed one after another in a line.

Bell Seat A rounded bell-shaped seat on Queen Anne chairs.

Bench A long seat, with or without a back.

Blanket Rack Frame on bracket feet with two or more crossbars.

Boat Bed Empire-style bed shaped like a gondola. A variant of the sleigh-bed.

Bonnet Top A broken arch pediment in tall furniture that covers the entire top from front to back.

Book Case Furniture style, usually with glass doors, open or revolving shelves, to store books.

Bow Front A convex curve on the front of a piece of furniture.

Box A closed receptacle with a lid.

Bracket A detachable wall fixture used to display a clock, candle stick, or china.

Bracket Foot A foot supporting a case piece, on each corner, consisting of two pieces of shaped wood joined at right angles, and applied to the underframing.

Broken Front Vertical breaks on the front surfaces of bookcases, etc.

Broken Pediment An opening in the centre of the pediment.

Buffet An open structure without doors of more than one tier, descended from the Elizabethan court cupboard.

Bureau A word for a desk with drawers.

Butler's Tray Serving tray mounted on folding X-frame stand.

Cabinet Glass-fronted case used for the display of china, glass, and *objets d'art*, also used for a rectangular piece of furniture with a two door cupboard with drawers above.

Cabriole Legs Curving leg used on chairs and other furniture. Sometimes with claw, pad or other style toes.

Camel back The curved or humped back of a sofa.

Candelabrum Table lighting appliance with more than one branch.

Candlestand A portable stand for a candlestick, candelabrum or lamp.

Caning A seat treatment from India using strips of cane instead of upholstery, introduced to the West Indies by the French and English. Light and airy, it was very popular and cool.

Canopy A term for an ornamental projection or suspended covering, usually over a four-poster bed.

Canterbury A small stand with partitions for music books. The name derives from one of the Archbishops of Canterbury, England.

Capital The top of a column or pilaster.

Carcass A name for the main structure of a piece of furniture.

Card Cut A cut-out design.

Card or Gaming Table A table with a felt or baize top.

Cartouche A fanciful scroll used sometimes as a finial or frame.

Case A box or chest.

Castors Wheels on the legs of tables, etc.

Cellaret A case with a lid on legs. The interior was separated to hold wine bottles.

Centre-Table Used in the middle of the drawing room, usually surrounded by rocking chairs.

Chair A stool with a back used throughout the house. They have many designs such as corner, saddle-back, elbow, arm, windsor, ladder-back, etc.

Chaise-Longue A one-ended sofa.

Channel Moulding A groove in the design usually on the edge.

Chamfer Bevelled edge, as when the sharp edges, or corners are cut off.

Chandelier A hanging fixture of several lights.

Checkers A design in squares.

Chest A box with a lid.

Chest of Drawers A box or chest with drawers that pull out in front.

Cheval Glass A standing mirror on four legs that swings between upright   supports.

Chiffonier A sideboard or low cupboard with shelves.

Chinese Style Designs from the East used in England from the 1600s.

Chintz Cotton with dyed designs from India and China, copied throughout Europe.

Chippendale Furniture A style in England by Thomas Chippendale, 1749–1822.

Claw and Ball Foot A design from the Chinese of a dragon claw holding a pearl at the foot of a cabriole leg. A very popular design in the eighteenth century.

Close or Night Stool A sanitary or toilet stool, sometimes called a commode or night table/stand.

Club Foot A leg resembling the head of a club.

Commode French usage for a chest of drawers or night stand. English usage for a night stand also.

Console A side-table with two legs that attaches to the wall or with four legs, the front two with a design.

Corbel A supporting bracket.

Cornice A moulded pattern forming the top of the entablature (q.v.).

Couch Another name for a daybed, sofa or lounge.

Court Cupboard A Medieval piece of furniture comprised of three open shelves, on carved and turned supports, the ancestor of the West Indian three-tiered open shelved sideboard.

Cradle A rocking child's bed.

Cresting The applied carving on the top of wardrobes, chairs, mirrors, cabinets, etc.

Cross-Stretcher X-shaped connector in straight or curved lines, between the four legs of a table or chair.

Cupboard Sideboard for display of silver and china, either open or with doors.

Day Bed Sofa with one or two ends, used to relax or sleep during the day.

Desk Style of furniture used for writing, reading or music, sometimes with a sloping top and drawers.

Dining-Table Round, oblong or square.

Document Drawer A thin narrow drawer in a desk for important papers.

Dowel Headless wooden pins used in construction.

Dressing Table A flat table with mirror for make-up and drawers for toiletries.

Drop Leaf Hinged extensions that can be raised to enlarge a table.

Dumb Waiter Dining-room stand, used near the dining-table, usually with three revolving circular trays on a tripod foot.

Egyptian Style A revival in the early nineteenth century of ancient North African motifs.

Empire Style French designs in the early nineteenth century.

Entablature The horizontal top superstructure in classical architecture.

Escutcheon A keyhole plate usually shield-shaped.

Evolutionary Pieces Antique furniture that has been restored and or renovated but not to its original state or usage, adding or deleting features.

Faux A French term for false, such as faux finishes on pine wood.

Feather Banding Two strips of veneer with diagonal graining to produce a herringbone design.

Fiddle Back A term to describe the feature resembling the outline of the musical instrument.

Finial A decorative terminal. Fluting Narrow vertical grooves used on columns of tables, or as a design on the sides of wardrobes.

Foot Stool A low furniture style for resting the legs.

Four-Poster The term used for a bedstead with four posts.

French Polish A method of applying a finish invented in France in the early nineteenth century.

Fretwork Perforated ornamentation.

Frieze The moulding under the entablature.

Gadrooning A carved ornamental edging of a repeated pattern, in an alternating series of concave and convex sections.

Gate Leg A swing-out feature that supports the drop leaf.

Gothic A style derived from the Goths in France.

Gothic Style Early medieval motifs at the foot of a cabriole leg. A sling bed, hanging between two posts.

Hall Table A piece of furniture used to receive incoming guests and goods.

Hammock A sling bed hanging between two posts.

Handkerchief A triangular table that opens up to form a square or a square table that opens in four to form a larger table.

Hepplewhite Furniture A style by George Hepplewhite in eighteenth century England, died 1786.

High or Tall Boy A unique piece of tall case furniture, in two pieces with drawers.

Horse Hair Mane and tail hair of the horse used in upholstered furniture.

Inlay The process of decorating a surface with varied woods.

Kneehole The space for knees when sitting at desks and dressers.

Knife Case A box to hold knives.

Lockplate Front plate used to protect the key hole.

Library Table A large table to spread out prints and maps.

Marquetry Design in veneer of rare and fine woods of the Rococo period of curving flowers and fancy scrolls.

Metal Mounts Metal designs used in furniture to protect vulnerable edges and hinges, locks, handles, etc.

Mortise and tenon The joining of two pieces of wood. The mortise is the cavity, the tenon is shaped to fill the cavity.

Moulding The shaped edge of a lid or cornice, etc.

Night Table Occasional table Small enclosed pot cupboard. Any light movable table, used for any occasion.

Ogee A double-curved moulding, convex above and concave below.

Ormolu French term used for gilded bronze mounts on furniture.

Painted Furniture Pine or other inexpensive woods decorated in different colours or designs.

Panel A board held together by surrounded frame-work of rails and stiles.

Parquetry Inlay of fine and rare woods using the straight, square, diamond and line designs.

Patina The aged original finish on furniture or other articles.

Pedestal The base of a column. Also used for the entire base column and cornice.

Pedestal Sideboard Furniture piece with two columns, cupboards and drawers, with centre connection.

Pediment The triangular-shaped termination over porticoes or the top of wardrobes, cabinets, etc.

Pembroke Table A small table with short drop leaves, also called a breakfast table. It is named after the Earl of Pembroke, as his wife was the first person to order this style.

Pendant A drop or hanging ornament.

Pie Safe A cupboard for food with mesh sides and doors for protection from insects.

Piecrust Table A round, tilt-top table on a tripod base. The top has a scalloped edge suggestive of a piecrust.

Pier Table Used under a mirror, usually between windows or in a hallway.

Pilaster A flattened column usually found on the sides of wardrobes.

Plinth The square member at the base of a column.

Press A wardrobe with shelves, usually employing weights such as covered bricks, to press down on the folded clothes after ironing to keep them smooth.

Rail Horizontal members on furniture such as chair tops.

Reeding Similar to fluting, but with the ornament in relief.

Regency Style English features during the Regency of George 1V, *circa* 1810–1830.

Rocking-Chair A chair mounted on rockers or runners. America and England claim invention of this style.

Rococo An ornate style developed in France from Chinese forms, also shells, scrolls, curving vines and flowers. Used from the eighteenth century onwards.

Rising Sun A fan-shaped ornament, half-circle motif.

Rosette A round ornament or motif in a floral design.

Roundel A circular ornament enclosing various designs.

Rum Table A reference to the piece of furniture used as a bar in the Antilles where rum, orange-juice, water, limes and sugar were mixed to make planters' and rum punches.

Runner The added strip on the bottom of drawers to make them slide easier.

Rush Seat A seat made from woven fibres.

Sabre Leg A term used to describe a sharply curving leg in the classical style.

Saddle Seat Shape carved into a wooden seat or an upholstered seat.

Screen Used to divide a room or hide the area in the bedroom used by the night stool.

Secretaire or Secretary The term used for 'writing furniture' with different compartments, with storage for books and papers.

Serpentine Shape Undulating curved surface or edges.

Settee A low wide seat for three or more, which developed similarly to the armchair.

Shelves Either hanging or standing, used for books, plates and china.

Sheraton Style Designs by Thomas Sheraton, England, 1751–1804.

Show Case Furniture for viewing art objects.

Sideboard Typical dining-room piece to display services of plate, china, glasses, etc. with drawers and storage spaces.

Sideboard Table A table to accommodate food during mealtimes.

Side Table For general usage in all rooms.

Slant-front desk An enclosed desk for writing, with the hinged lid sloping at a forty-five degree angle, when closed.

Sleigh bed An Empire or Regency bed shaped like a sleigh.

Sofa A wide chair or day bed, to seat three or more.

Sofa table Rectangular and narrow table with two front drawers in the apron, and hinged leaves at each end. It is used in the front or back of the sofa.

Spanish Foot A furniture foot with vertical ribs, somewhat like a hand resting on its knuckles.

Splat The vertical centre of a chair back, sometimes pierced.

Staining The colouring of light woods to resemble darker varieties.

Stands Used for candles and plants, etc.

Stile Vertical members of framework.

Stool Backless seat used for dressing tables or in front of arm chairs to support the sitter's legs, etc.

Strapwork Interlaced ornamentation.

Stretchers Rails used to unite chairs and table legs, etc.

Stringing or inlay Narrow band of wood used for contrasting decoration String in inlay work.

Tea Table Usually round, square or folded and used for the ritual of tea drinking.

Tea Caddy Small boxes (usually lockable) for holding tea, an expensive commodity, in the eighteenth century.

Teapoy Small table for holding tea canisters.

Tip-top A table feature that allows the hinged top to go from horizontal to vertical for storage.

Toilet Mirror A small mirror, often on a case, with a drawer, designed to stand on a table or chest of drawers.

Towel Rack Small stand with three crossbars.

Trays Boards with rims to hold glasses, plates, tea equipage, etc.

Tripod Tables and Stands Furniture with centre columns on three legs.

Tulip Ornament Formalized flower-form feature, inspired by designs from Holland and Persia.

Turning Shaped wood done on a lathe.

Upholstery The covering of seated furniture with stuffing and materials.

Universal Table Folding, swivel-top tables that are used for tea, cards or games.

Varnish A finish used to protect the wooden surface.

Veneer Thin sheets of precious wood applied to a less precious one to   improve the appearance of the piece.

Wash stand Adapted for bedroom use after 1780, there are two versions: either a high, four-legged table with a drawer and back-splash with spindle gallery or with a hole in the top for the basin, a drawer on the bottom shelf and towel rails on the sides.

Whatnot A shelved stand, in many styles and ornaments.

Wheat ears Low-carved relief, introduced by Hepplewhite.

Wine Cisterns A metal-lined container for keeping bottled drinks cool.

Work table Made for ladies' needlework, etc.

Writing Fall-front furniture enclosing a system of small drawers cabinet and a writing space, usually covered in leather.

Writing or Reading table Small, folding top-table that opens to a forty-five degree table for the resting of papers or books.

Furniture Index

(Page numbers in **bold** refer to illustrations)

GENERAL INDEX

(Page numbers in **bold** refer to illustrations)

ISLANDS OF THE WEST INDIES

(Mentioned in the text)
(Page numbers in **bold** refer to illustrations)